JUSTICE

First, I want to point out that Julian Assange knew how 9/11 was critical to what was happening and what was to follow. We saw that in November 2009 he was still troubled by the 9/11 event because everything that was happening goes back to this event. I will argue that the government can't choose to ignore 9/11 because all the materials they are complaining about everything only started because of 9/11. In Nov 2009 Wikileaks released 570000 pager messages which were sent on 9/11.

Why? This is the trigger of the Existing, Clear, and Present Danger. The government had not even contained this threat 9 years later as Osama Bin Laden was still at large. So, this triggered the need to do something about this before the terrorists strike again. We believe he knew that the government was still at it again [the terrorists attributed 9/11 to having been triggered by the government's reckless foreign policy]. This triggered the need to Escalate in order to De-escalate and so he published the video of possible war crimes. The intended recipient was the government itself. Exercising his rights to hold the government to account where it is the one outsourcing terror. 3000 people were dead, so this was not something to take lightly.

But this might have triggered the Obama administration into action as well or at least opened the need for public debate about the issue.

- ***Aug. 30, 2010***: *In an Oval Office address, President Barack Obama declares an end to U.S. combat operations in Iraq.*
- ***May 2, 2011***: *Osama bin Laden is killed by U.S. special operations forces during a raid at an Abbottabad, Pakistan compound.*
- ***June 22, 2011***: *In a televised address, Obama announces a withdrawal of U.S. troops from Afghanistan and a handover of power to Afghani security by 2014.*

Mind you they took 9 years to act. The publications of the material can be attributed to having invigorated the government to resolve the outstanding issues. More leaks about how the FBI and CIA operate made them feel exposed. Probably they were hoping to eliminate Osama Bin Laden digitally using a drone etc as they emphasized methodology instead of doing the actual job. By May 2011 doing it manually; Osama Bin Laden was dead.

The Existing, Clear, and Present Danger was now eliminated, and the threat was now contained.

Even if it is a coincidence, remember it took 9 years before anything materialized. After the release and publication of the materials within six months to a year the threat had been contained.

This is a fact no matter what the government wants you to believe and this proves that Julian Assange and all journalists and publishers out there are part and parcel of an effective democratic system that puts checks in place to hold the government accountable. As no one is above the law. The deaths of 3000 civilians due to the government's foreign policy meant that the government had lost its right to stand for the people as it was them whose actions were putting the lives of the people at risk. Now in the journalist's shoes it's even worse because people have died. Therefore, could not rely on the Espionage Act. The guilty part of the government of having had 3000 civilians killed made the Espionage Act on Assange null and void and this was replaced by the First Amendment Act that gave Assange the right to hold the government accountable as they are the ones who were threats to the citizens. But a lot of things were misunderstood. I am going to argue that the message [publications] was meant for the government and not any foreign government. Secondly, the publications highlighted possible war crimes, but the fact that Assange didn't lodge a case with the courts meant that all he wanted was to get the issues resolved and let the government put its house in order through the Escalate to De-escalate approach.

We believe that the government took the stance it did to protect its soldiers. But years have passed now, and every country involved has protected its soldiers and twenty years

FREE JULIAN ASSANGE

Escalate-to-Deescalate

Magna Carta. Clause 39 & 40

"No free man shall be seized, imprisoned, dispossessed, outlawed, exiled or ruined in any way, nor in any way proceeded against, except by the lawful judgement of his peers and the law of the land."
"To no one, will we sell, to no one will we deny or delay right or justice."
messages it claims were sent on Sept. 11, 2001.

*2009 **November:** WikiLeaks posts more than half-a-million pager messages it claims were sent on Sept. 11, 2001.*

I think there is no analysis of the Wikileaks founder, his acts of publishing information, and the Espionage Act without looking at the 9/11 terror attacks. 9/11 is the trigger of what follows. 9/11 rewrote the laws.

Ladies and gentlemen, I introduce the new laws to protect investigative journalists and publishers.
Introducing the Existing, Clear, and Present Danger Act.

Tomorrow's World Order's Perspective

David Gomadza

ISBN: 978-1-4709-4942-6

on no one has been brought to court. That means also Assange must be freed. It is not justice for a reporter, an investigative journalist or publisher to be held in a maximum-security prison when those who violated international law walk free.
We are not saying that your boys and girls must stand trial. No. We are saying that it's time to drop all charges and free Assange.
To open the floor, I will quote Amnesty International's Secretary General Agnes Callamard.

"The US government's pursuit of Julian Assange for having published and disclosed documents that included possible war crimes by the US military is nothing short of a full-scale assault on the right to freedom of expression."

Wikileaks publishes 570000 messages capturing chaos of 9/11

https://www.theguardian.com › media › nov › wikileak...

25 Nov 2009 — **Wikileaks** publishes 570,000 messages capturing chaos of **9/11** ... The mental and emotional storm that struck America on 11 September 2001 with the ...
You've visited this page many times. Last visit: 08/12/22

Wikileaks publishes September 11 pager messages

https://www.theguardian.com › world › blog › nov › se...

25 Nov 2009 — The unfolding secret story of the **9/11** attacks on the World Trade Centre and the Pentagon is being told today when more than 500,000 ...

WikiLeaks publishes intercepted 9/11 pager messages

https://www.france24.com › France 24 › Business

27 Nov 2009 — Scoop hunting website **WikiLeaks** has released 570,000 pager messages sent in the United States on the day the World Trade Centre collapsed, ...
You visited this page on 08/12/22.

FREE JULIAN ASSANGE

GOVERNMENT ACCOUNTABILITY

11 September 2001

This day changed the world.

9/11 rewrote the rules.

9/11 rewrote the laws.
9/11 restructured the system.
9/11 reversed liability and accountability roles.

9/11 rendered the Espionage Act null and void.

You can't talk about Wikileaks without talking
about 9/11
You cant talk about the Espionage Act without
talking about 9/11

It is a sad reality but 9/11 rewrote the laws. 9/11 changed the rules. 9/11 changed the game and it's a fact, things will never be the same again.

1. But out of all this dark age in history, something new came out. 9/11 created an opportunity for humanity to rewrite the laws.
2. Ladies and gentlemen, I introduce the new laws to protect investigative journalists and publishers.
3. **Introducing the Existing, Clear, and Present Danger Act.**
4. 9/11 did not affect America only but the whole world. Surely 9/11 changed the lives of many around the world.
5. I believe that this was and is still an opportunity to change the laws and perceptions. As I have advocated throughout. 9/11 did not kill the American people only.
6. It murdered the Espionage Act as well. 9/11 opened a platform to rewrite these laws. It shifted power from the government who outsourced terror with its reckless foreign policy of triggering wars. To investigative journalists and publishers who are now the guardians of humanity. Now entrusted with the task of acting as checks and powers to scrutinize the government and through the Escalate-to-De Escalate create a platform for encouraging debates and

holding the government accountable where their actions have caused the deaths of its own citizens on its own soil. Meaning caught off guard hence the need for this new group of overseers. The ones who have the safety of the people and the continued existence of humanity at heart. It has become apparent that the Espionage Act to some extent has become irrelevant given the kind of threats terrorism introduced. Surely the global political tensions and the risks of a nuclear war mean forever we shall need these investigative journalists and publishers. Even now humanity is at it again going back to the 1665-1667 Anglo-Dutch war and using that script in the Russia and Ukraine proxy war [Read our prediction].

7. https://play.google.com/store/audiobooks/details?id=AQA AAEBCXEgcGM&gl=GB

8. I think there is no analysis of the Wikileaks founder, his acts of publishing information, and the Espionage Act without looking at the 9/11 terror attacks. 9/11 is the trigger of what follows. Therefore, relying on the Espionage Act and disregarding 9/11 is not just immoral but an attack on personal liberties and freedoms. As such it would be unfair to judge Julian Assange without looking at 9/11.

9. 9/11 meant the need for a new system of checks and scrutiny of the government. Not necessarily because the government is corrupt no, but because we have a new form of threats in terrorism. Above all, they could not even anticipate the terror. Everyone was caught off guard. Hence the need for proactive checks. We, therefore, argue that going after investigative journalists and publishers is an 'assault on freedom of speech'.

10. Surely, I believe no one would want to see 9/11 ever again.

11. But the fact that the current system suppresses justice is suspicious.

12. This is a chance to introduce new settings, new thinking, and new laws that fit today's circumstances. The fact that you go back to the 1660s for answers is disturbing.

13. 9/11 shifted the blame from the investigative journalist to the government. All the harm the journalists can do is tell the world the truth and what the government does is take the law into its own hands and outsource terror. Killing own people simply because they can and anyone who complains will spend years without a fair trial in prison.
14. But is this justice?
15. I will tell you what justice is.
16. Your reliance on the Espionage Act was nulled and voided by 9/11 events.
17. Ladies and gentlemen introducing the laws that will protect Investigative Journalists and all publishers; the Existing, Clear, and Present Danger Act.
18. When they wrote the Espionage Age surely governments then were angels. It was absurd to even think that governments would kill their citizens or contribute to such acts. To make things worse on their soil. So, this Espionage Act was fitting to safeguard the lives of the people. But I ask you, can you say the same thing today that governments are innocent?
19. Even if not directly linked they must do more to protect their citizens. The fact that they suppress channels of help through these investigative journalists is suspect.
20. Terrorism has meant the need for new laws. The need to incorporate these journalists and publishers into the system. They are the crucial missing link that provides the checks and scrutinizes the government.
21. We believe that they have a role to play to protect citizens. The enemies have become much wiser than the governments. Therefore, you need these players.
22. Hence it is fitting to take the lead and show you the way.
23. Let's give them the benefit of the doubt.
24. Let's protect them as well.
25. Okay, not all can be angels.
26. But if there is an Existing, Clear, and Present Danger Act that is linked to the government's own dealing with others through their foreign policy.
27. It is fair. If your hands are clean, then do what you want with them.

A New World Order.
Signed 08 December 2022.
The First Global President
David Gomadza
00447863020828
info@twofuture.world
www.twofuture.world

28. Tomorrow's World Order Journalist, Publisher's Freedom Charter.

29. For argument's sake, this is our working hypothesis. The framework we are going to use as a guideline to argue that journalists and publishers are part and parcel of the fabric of democracy. They have roles to play to safeguard the lives of the citizens unlike what the government claims to be the case. That they put lives in danger.

30. The funny thing about all this is that they only arise only after a terrible Existing, Clear and Present Danger. In most cases triggered by the actions of the government. Who trigger this through their foreign policy of outsourcing terror and through reckless dealings abroad? The interesting fact here is the fact that roles are reversed once the civilians have been murdered due to the actions of the government. The government will have lost the ability to stand on behalf of the people and use the Espionage Act to protect the people. Now it is their actions that have caused the deaths of civilians.

31. Their reckless foreign policy of indirectly outsourcing terror as with 9/11 is the source of the Existing, Clear, and Present Danger. One that makes the Espionage Act null and void. Rendering the government unable to claim that they are protecting the lives of the people. 9/11 is the source of

what happened years later. 9/11 set up a chain of events that triggered the rise of the real defenders of civilians, the investigative journalists and the publishers. The people's guardian angels who are to challenge the government. As well as to hold them accountable for their actions to prevent further harm from befalling the civilians.

32. They are to expose the evil acts of the government in an escalate-to-de-escalate approach. But a lot of things are misunderstood at this stage. I must state that the intended recipient of the released and published classified documents is the government itself.

33. They published the material to exercise their rights guaranteed by the First Amendment. The government will have lost its right to use the Espionage Act as it is the one that would have caused the death of civilians. To make things worse on its own soil. This triggers the need for those able to put a platform in place to rise and provide the conditions that will be used to scrutinize the government.

34. I will argue that 9/11 is the trigger of what followed for at least a decade after the incident. So, to assess Julian Assange's case we must first look at this dreadful event that even triggered the war and everything the government is using to justify its charges. So, 9/11 is what set the ball rolling. I will prove that the release of the material and its publication help to resolve some of the issues that could have worsened the situation and increased the likely chances of harm to the people.

35. The act of releasing and publishing material is part of a strategy which I will refer to as the Escalate to de-escalate and contain. Meaning they actually helped to protect the lives of the American people. They highlighted to the government what their soldiers were doing abroad. Still committing what could amount to war crimes. It is they and their actions that triggered the need for dialogue and the resolutions of the outstanding issues.

36. In other words, they highlighted the need to contain the immediate; Existing, Clear, and Present danger in Osama Bin laden. This a reminder to the government not to forget

9/11 but to act fast. They opened the debate to discuss war crimes.

37. I will argue throughout that their actions did not introduce new material but just highlighted what everyone knew already. After all, the courts and other bodies would have requested the materials anywhere soon or later. So, their release and publication is not material to this case.

38. Mind you Osama Bin Laden in 2010 was still at large. But here is the great part of this case. The timeline of their release of the material and its publications and the resolution of all outstanding issues coincides.

39. *2009*

40. ***November:*** *WikiLeaks posts more than half-a-million pager messages it claims were sent on Sept. 11, 2001.*

41. *2010*

42. ***April:*** *WikiLeaks posts a classified U.S. military video of a U.S. Apache helicopter gunship firing on what the military says were believed to be armed fighters in New Baghdad, Iraq. Among the 18 killed were two Reuters journalists.*

43. ***May:*** *Pfc. Bradley (later known as Chelsea) Manning is arrested by the U.S. military and then court-martialed in June, charged with leaking the combat video posted on WikiLeaks as well as classified State Department documents by downloading those documents to a personal computer.*

44. ***July:*** *WikiLeaks posts what it calls "The Afghan War Logs," more than 75,000 classified documents that record previously undisclosed civilian casualties inflicted by the U.S. and coalition forces, details of the pursuit of Osama bin Laden and accounts of stepped-up fighting by the Taliban.*

45. ***August:*** *WikiLeaks founder Julian Assange faces an arrest warrant over allegations of rape and molestation during a visit to Sweden; police question him in Stockholm, where he denies the allegations.*

46. ***October:*** *WikiLeaks posts nearly 400,000 classified military documents it calls "The Iraq War Logs"; they detail the involvement of Iraqi security forces in the torture*

of prisoners of war, document higher civilian death tolls, and describe Iran's support for Iraqi insurgents.

47. ***November:*** *WikiLeaks posts the first 250,000 of more than 3 million leaked U.S. diplomatic cables from nearly 300 American consulates and embassies worldwide that span the years from 1966 to 2010.*

48. ***December:*** *Assange is arrested in London to face extradition for the Swedish allegations; he is released and put under house arrest after posting bail.*

49. *2011*

50. ***February:*** *WikiLeaks posts seven cables from the U.S. Embassy in Cairo, amid violent clashes between Egyptian security forces and pro-democracy demonstrators; the documents discuss Egypt's human rights and civil liberties violations.*

51. ***April:*** *WikiLeaks posts "The Guantanamo Files," some 800 classified military documents detailing the official allegations of terrorist actions by the men held captive in Guantanamo Bay, Cuba.*

52. https://www.npr.org/2019/04/11/712306713/12-years-of-disruption-a-wikileaks-timeline

53. First, I want to point out that Julian Assange knew how 9/11 was critical to what was happening and what was to follow. We saw that in November 2009 he was still troubled by the 9/11 event because everything that was happening goes back to this event. I will argue that the government can't choose to ignore 9/11 because all the materials they are complaining about everything only started because of 9/11. In Nov 2009 he released 500000 pager messages which were sent on 9/11.

54. Why? This is the trigger of the Existing, Clear, and Present Danger. The government had not even contained this threat 9 years later as Osama Bin Laden was still at large. So, this triggered the need to do something about this before the terrorists strike again. We believe he knew that the government was still at it again [the terrorists attributed 9/11 to having been triggered by the government's reckless

foreign policy]. This triggered the need to Escalate in order to de-escalate and so he published the video of possible war crimes. The intended recipient was the government itself. Exercising his rights to hold the government to account where it is the one outsourcing terror. 3000 people were dead, so this was not something to take lightly.

55. But this might have triggered the Obama administration into action as well or at least opened the need for public debate about the issue.

- *Aug. 30, 2010: In an Oval Office address, President Barack Obama declares an end to U.S. combat operations in Iraq.*
- *May 2, 2011: Osama bin Laden is killed by U.S. special operations forces during a raid at an Abbottabad, Pakistan compound.*
- *June 22, 2011: In a televised address, Obama announces a withdrawal of U.S. troops from Afghanistan and a handover of power to Afghani security by 2014.*

56. In April 2010 Wikileaks published *the U.S. military video of a U.S. Apache helicopter gunship firing on what the military says were believed to be armed fighters in New Baghdad, Iraq.*

57. Followed by files in July The Afghan War Logs.

58. By August 2010 the Obama Administration had announced the withdrawal of troops from Iraq.

59. Mind you they took 9 years to act. The publications of the material can be attributed to having invigorated the government to resolve the outstanding issues. More leaks about how the FBI and CIA operate made them feel exposed. Probably they were hoping to eliminate Osama Bin Laden digitally using a drone etc as they emphasized methodology instead of doing the actual job. By May 2011 doing it manually; Osama Bin Laden was dead.

60. The Existing, Clear, and Present Danger was now eliminated, and the threat was now contained.

61. Even if it is a coincidence, remember it took 9 years before anything materialized. After the release and publication of

the materials within six months to a year the threat had been contained.

62. This is a fact no matter what the government wants you to believe and this proves that Julian Assange and all journalists and publishers out there are part and parcel of an effective democratic system that puts checks in place to hold the government accountable. As no one is above the law. The deaths of 3000 civilians due to the government's foreign policy meant that the government had lost its right to stand for the people as it was them whose actions were putting the lives of the people at risk. Now in the journalist's shoes it's even worse because people have died.

63. Therefore, could not rely on the Espionage Act. The guilty part of the government of having had 3000 civilians killed made the Espionage Act on Assange null and void and this was replaced by the First Amendment Act that gave Assange the right to hold the government accountable as they are the ones who were threats to the citizens. But a lot of things were misunderstood. I am going to argue that the message [publications] was meant for the government and not any foreign government. Secondly, the publications highlighted possible war crimes, but the fact that Assange didn't lodge a case with the courts meant that all he wanted was to get the issues resolved and let the government put its house in order through the Escalate to De-escalate approach.

64. We believe that the government took the stance it did to protect its soldiers. But years have passed now, and every country involved has protected its soldiers and twenty years on no one has been brought to court. That means also Assange must be freed. It is not justice for a reporter, an investigative journalist or publisher to be held in a maximum-security prison when those who violated international law walk free.

65. We are not saying that your boys and girls must stand trial. No. We are saying that it's time to drop all charges and free Assange.

66. To open the floor, I will quote Amnesty International's Secretary General Agnes Callamard.

67. "The US government's pursuit of Julian Assange for having published and disclosed documents that included possible war crimes by the US military is nothing short of a full-scale assault on the right to freedom of expression."

68. After all the Magna Carta is still in force in the UK clauses 39 states that.

69. *"No free man shall be seized, imprisoned, dispossessed, outlawed, exiled or ruined in any way, nor in any way proceeded against, except by the lawful judgement of his peers and the law of the land."*

70. *"To no one, will we sell, to no one will we deny or delay right or justice."*

71. *UK parliament laws. Magna Carta.*

72. Tomorrow's World Order Journalist, Publisher's Freedom Charter.

73. Journalist and publishers' Freedom laws.

74. We as Tomorrow's World Order. We must ensure that a country's justice system, president, prime minister, cult, or any leader, etc is not above the law. This is in line with the need to uphold the concepts of freedom and equality under the law.

75. Escalate to De-escalate.

76. Journalists and publishers are now protected by our laws as they are critical to the survival of humanity at large. Given the ever-rising threats posed by wars, nuclear weapons, and terrorist acts among other things.

77. The continuous making of nuclear weapons and the forever-rise in global tension evidenced by the risks of a

nuclear war posed by the Russia and Ukraine war highlights the presence of existential threats to all humanity.

78. As such journalists and producers of information etc are now tasked with greater responsibilities of safeguarding humanity at large. These groups of people have obligations and duties placed upon them to be involved in acts that fall in the Escalate-to-De-escalate situation as a corrective proactive action to safeguard humanity at large.

79. This is because they have roles to pinpoint government actions that pose risks to all humanity. Actions that bring harm to its own citizens. Journalists, publishers, etc must publish material without fear of being unlawfully imprisoned or detained.

80. There must be proof or reasonable grounds to believe that the government concerned is outsourcing terror that is putting risks to the lives of its own citizens.

81. There must be a direct or indirect link between say a country's foreign policy and the atrocities suffered by its own citizens.

82. The government must be in violation of the human rights of its citizens.

83. To be justified there must be probable grounds to suspect that it is the government's actions that are responsible for the harm suffered by its own citizens.

84. This might not hold water where it can't be proved that government actions have a direct or indirect impact on the harm being suffered or that which the people have already suffered.

85. The idea is to protect national security as well as to avoid malicious publications of government secrets where there are no prospects of proving that it is doing anything that puts the citizens at risk of harm or death.

86. Evidence of past harm to a country's own citizens or people living where the same government has control can suffice.

87. Before publishing, there must be evidential grounds in an IF-THEN casual effect that it's the government's actions or foreign policy that is bringing harm to its own people.
88. Ascertain whether you can prove a causal-effect link between the government's actions, or its foreign policy and the harm suffered already or likely to be suffered.
89. Past harm to the government's own citizens gives the case more compelling grounds than just accusations of violations of human rights.

90. The atrocities suffered must be of high magnitude.

91. Must have been suffered by a lot of people.
92. Must have been so traumatic so as to leave people temporarily incapacitated to make sound decisions. This is because after this event fears influence the decisions people make after that.
93. The culprits or suspects who caused the event at the time of publication must still be at large and the threat not contained. Meaning that the threat still presents and is imminent unless contained. This is in line with the Existing, Clear, and Present danger theory. The events must have occurred in the past but have not been contained and the initial triggers of the event are even amplified at the time of publications mainly due to the recklessness of the government whose acts even if not intentional are putting people's lives at risk.
94. Presence of and involvement of a government's ally or partner who is working together with the government. This can be one of the grounds to justify publications and the release of classified material. That release and publication, etc would be likely to reveal malicious acts by the government's ally who might have vested interests, competing for interest, or just the two grouping together to perform an illegal act so that it is easy to cover up.
95. Any illegal dealings especially on the part of the government's ally like the falsifying of dossiers, misrepresentations of facts. Skipping of clearly defined needed steps, and laws e.g. skipping the need to get a UN

resolution or permit by the responsible body before going to war.

96. The country's corruption status, presence of other threats to the government, other existential threats, and recent events like the pandemic and wars can agument a case and make a case deserves more scrutiny.

97. Debt owed between these allies must be assessed as this could be the trigger of malicious acts. For example, it would be easy to convince a country you owe money to embark on an illegal war promising it to repay the debt with the confiscated resources.

98. Threats of war crimes investigations by international law courts can contribute to the pressures too.

99. Assess any previous requests through the freedom of information Act.

100. Obviously guilty on the part of the ally of the government if it is in a tight financial position which can lead to wrongful acts.

101. Publications of documents must be in the public interest or that of holding the government to account and not for profit. This is because the publications will benefit the public in an Escalate-to-De-escalate situation. That will lead to an inquiry, independent investigation, or another government getting involved to scrutinise it.

102. The initial aim behind publication here is not to take the government to court. But publish for the government so they become aware of the acts of their soldiers in order to effect a change in practices that in turn will safeguard the lives of the people.

103. It must be stated that the initial intention is not to get the government into trouble, otherwise it is simply going to take a defensive stance and attack as the best form of defence. Which can mean unlawful imprisonment for years without a trial.

104. The publication can also help put pressure on the government to act swiftly or put more resources to aim to

get the leaders or masterminds of the atrocities who at this time might still be at large.

105.   The atrocities must have occurred on the country's or government's soil and not abroad.

106.   Or they are likely to happen on country's soil?

107.   If the government has an ally, assess whether there are different laws related to the case. For example, the Magna Carta which safeguards the rights of citizens by giving citizens the right to hold the government accountable for its actions is still law and in force in England, especially Clauses 39 & 40. But the same act is not applicable and not law in the US.

108.   Where the two nations form a treaty to trap and prosecute journalists. If a journalist escapes persecution from one country without the safeguards given by the Magna Carta e.g. the US to one with the safeguard e.g. the UK. Instead of the country with safeguards to give that journalist political asylum. The government of that country goes on to imprison that journalist without being charged but simply on the belief that an extradition order will be requested.

109.   Where a country is involved too as in this case the UK being an ally of the US who have gone to war together. A journalist that escapes to this country must be treated as a political asylum as they are involved as well, they lose the right to hold the journalist for any extradition orders. The 'holding country' can only apply its local laws if the journalist is found innocent and must be released if wrongfully imprisoned and must be compensated.

110.   No extradition request will apply in this case where the two countries are allies and have both committed the alleged atrocities. All extradition requests between the two countries shall be null and void.

111.   The chicken egg saga.

112.   Dates of publication and dates the event happened must be clearly stated. No notions of futuristic predictions. A good example is when country A falsifies dossiers that

are used to justify going to war simply because they will entice some loyal people through the pledges of allegiance in the future to leak classified documents and give them protection. Thereby claiming that the leaked documents in this case. An event that happened after the invasion. To them is the reason why they went to war in the first place. As they had foreseen this. They can argue that they knew at some point in time in the future that this leak would happen anyway. So, going to war now or in the future would not change the issues at hand. Then breach all international laws.

113.   To cover their evil acts of falsifying dossiers they unlawfully hold the journalists and producers who published materials, aiming to get rid of these unjustly.

114.   The time that has elapsed.

115.   Could the same information if requested by other bodies and international courts could have been released at some point in time in the future?

116.   If issues related to wars or military operations then it follows that there would be an investigation of war crimes etc anyway at some point in the future meaning publications especially of already well known facts cannot become material to justify holding a person for a long period in prison.

117.   An assessment of demands by the government on pledges of allegiance.

118.   Governments can simply be strict with journalists and publishers who are not fully of that nation. Simply because they expect loyalty no matter what and as such a way to show power as violations of allegiances are taken seriously as they are regarded as acts of rebellion. This means the government will be tougher on an Australian-American rather than on an American- American. Common

in countries with monarchies where any rebellion is classified as treason.

119.   Can it be proved that the government is cheating or using outdated practices?

120.   For example, going back in time using the script then say from the 1665-1667 Anglo-Dutch war and replicate the events then by triggering a proxy war where Ukraine fights Russia on behalf of the West.

121.   All this is for the West to be able to predict and influence the course of history. In which cases the journalist or publisher is protected by our laws because such acts are not only inhuman as they strip away hard-earned freedoms and personal liberties. It doesn't matter if the government's intentions are in good faith or not. The fact that they are using outdated scripts makes them suspects.

122.   Did people have personal liberties then like we have today? Is the litmus test. This helps to justify the need to hold the government to account where its acts have already caused the deaths of its people; the publisher or journalist simply needs to prove that the government is going back in time for solutions. That mindset means that the government can't be trusted to do right as they are triggering a war that is killing women and children.

123.   What if Russia is to find out? That can make them shell the West as well. So, the journalist or publisher would be exonerated given that Russia has intercontinental ballistic nuclear weapons. This and their support for the war and the heavy deaths of Russian soldiers increased the risks of a nuclear war. So, there is an Existing, Clear Presence or futuristic threat. So publishing is in the interest of humanity to hold the government to account in an Escalate-to De-escalated case. The risks of nuclear war can justify the release of classified material and their publications.

124.   Any historical feuds, ransoms, treason charges of the past, etc?

125.   These issues can justify the need to publish materials. Could the British be mistaking Assange for George Washington? Assange stepped into the shoes of the founders and highlighted Britain's oppressive dealings. That it was killing its people or acting unjustly. Now America admits that the founders were wrong, and that Britain should have imprisoned them under the treason Act [Espionage Age] as they are Adamant that Julian Assange is guilty.

126.   This means that the British still own America which they leased to the founders on a long-term lease just as they did with the Chagos island. The British have put Assange in George Washington's footsteps and secretly they are holding him for treason. Marked to die in a maximum-security prison just to show the US power. The US just because Assange does not subscribe to the pledges of allegiance because he is part Australian doesn't care about him. In Australia people are taught to fight to correct a wrong. He exposed the government only as exercising his rights to hold the government to account where it can be proved that it's the government that is the enemy of the people and not the journalists or publishers

127.   So, the US don't care as they insist on Espionage Act charges even after pardoning their own. Even after all international courts have dropped charges against the British and the USA.

128.   That begs the question that; does Assange know more than he published? Clauses 39 and 40 of the Magna Carta are still in force in Britain which means they should have not held him in prison. I think it is absurd that they keep him in a maximum-security prison all in the hope that an extradition order would come through.

129.   What is Britain covering up? Does Assange have anything against Britain? Could Britain be involved in the 9/11 terror acts on America? Is Britain blackmailing the USA? But why even suggest Britain's involvement in 9/11?

Britain might be saying that George Washington and the founding father did the same to Britain. If the USA considers Assange guilty it follows too that the founders were guilty of treason [Espionage Act exposing the King's tax system, which they regarded as corrupt and harming the people] as such America belongs to Britain. To prove a point Britain acquired Chagos and drove everyone out and gave this Chagos to the US on a long-term lease fifty plus years.

130.   To prove the point that the founders were wrong to revolt, the British are going to hold Assange forever, so he dies for the founding fathers who they regard as having committed treason.

131.   The issue of squatters in Chagos case was eliminated by the 9/11 attacks as the FBI and CIA established an interrogation base there after 9/11.

132.   The 9/11 flight plane paths depict the Chagos map. The airports of original flights correspond with the first 5 colonies.

133.   Britain is so digitally advanced that they can implant a chip in everyone at birth. One they will use to replay voice recordings with low-volume sounds. After recording a person's voice through these chips. If the person is religious, enough. When they play the sound at low decibels in the inner ear the brain on matching the person's voice converts the audio into images so that if in deep sleep the person might think that he was dreaming. What if they whisper to the person who is in deep sleep; that the person goes to the USA and kills people? If religious enough to believe in a God or Allah he might actually go and kill. After all, all 9/11 terrorists were known to the authorities. Meaning what? They were being tortured remotely through the chip, drone technology in humans, and remote electromagnetic nerve tampering to breaking points that only revenge becomes the ultimate solution?

134.   Maybe this theory doesn't hold water?

135.   Okay, what if they are recreating the 1660s? What if 9/11 was the creation of the Great Fire of London of 1666

with Larry Silverstone the owner of the World Trade Centre Towers playing Christopher Wren a famous British 'jerk of all trades' from the 1660s? The same man who designed the plans that were used to build New York.

136.   Which was named after the brother of the king he served James I Duke of York. To make things even more interesting the same architect who designed the building-plans used in building the twin towers. The same man who incorporated the idea of the time-ball into buildings. A technique that then, was used to predict time so that the ship captain can tell the time.

137.   The same idea was used to build World Trade Centre 3 that free fell. Would you be surprised at the number of controversies that surrounded the free falling of World Trade Centre Three? Especially now you know that this was what they used to do in the 1660s in order to tell time. They would place a huge ball on the rooftop as part of the building and then simply pull the lever on the pulley system incorporated in the building so that the ball free fell.

138.   But did you know that Christopher Wren was the first architect to use gunpowder, namely 3 kg to lift 3000 kg marbles of stone in the air from St Paul's Cathedral wall? A religious person who knows about Sodom and Gomorrah where God destroyed the corrupt merchants who were doing inside trading with sulphur and fire from the skies. Now picture planes [aluminium] filled with jet fuel burning as demolition agents.

139.   Do you know that the same man introduced the colony collapse syndrome strategy where he experimented with bees using his design with buttress columns with glass, he put bees in an enclosure and introduced smoke? He noticed that bees even if there was an escape route down would fly up to escape the smoke to their deaths. Picture people stuck at the top levels of the world trade center. Okay maybe still not convinced.

140.   The same man introduced the idea of the Guantanamo bay cages through the colony collapse syndrome strategy. Where he observed that if male bees are removed and put in an enclosure with see-through glass.

The other bees won't react, but the young males fail to feed or provide food to the rest of the colony and in the end the colony collapses. Picture Guantanamo cages with people being put in the enclosures for decades without any charges brought on them.

141.   Now, this is the final piece to the puzzle to rule out this as a coincidence. Google the pictures of Christopher Wren 1660s and that of Larry Silverstone the owner of the World Trade Centre in 2001.

142.   Exactly the same person; spitting-image.

143.   But how do they achieve this?

144.   Recreating past events by using that script and looking for identical people as they have paintings of every player then. A requirement they started as far back as 1066.

145.   To prove this, we published the Russian-Ukraine War Prediction using the 1665-1667 Anglo-Dutch War. Just check the accuracy of our prediction first. Free download.

146.   https://play.google.com/store/books/details/David_Gomadza_A_Perfect_Prediction_Russia_Ukraine?id=PmaVEAAAQBAJ&gl=GB

147.   Event after event.

148.   I went as far as this so that you understand that freeing Assange involves more than waiting for the courts.

149.   The first step is petitioning the President, Prime Minister, or King as the first start. If you wait for the court system forever, he will be in prison.

150.   This is not justice.

151.   We can expose these absurd acts of looking for answers from the 1660s and rewrite history our way. A new world order.

152.   I covered a lot of issues in this book.

153.   Is Britain holding Assange for the US's interests or holding him to keep him quiet? Surely, he might know something no one else knows, otherwise he should be a free man.

154.   The Magna Carta which is still in force in England especially clauses 39 and 40 states that.

155.   *"No free man shall be seized, imprisoned, dispossessed, outlawed, exiled or ruined in any way, nor in any way proceeded against, except by the lawful judgement of his peers and the law of the land.*
156.   *"To no one, will we sell, to no one will we deny or delay right or justice."*
157.   *UK parliament laws. Magna Carta.*

158.   Yet Assange is still in prison without any charges.

159.   READ ALL UNTIL THE LAST PAGE.

160.   NOW THAT YOU KNOW SOMETHING NEW HOW CAN YOU HELP TO FREE ASSANGE?
161.   Do whatever you can. He should be out by Christmas.
162.   Let us start afresh.
163.   I am the new First Global President
164.   David Gomadza.
165.   00447863020828
166.   Info@twofuture.world
167.   www.twofuture.world

168.   Existing, Clear, and Present Danger.
169.   *: a risk or threat to safety or other public interests that is serious and imminent*
170.   *especially: one that justifies the limitation of a right (such as freedom of speech or press) by the legislative or executive branch of government.*

171.   Breach of this if a citizen can see the government use the Espionage Act. But what if it's the government who is posing a risk to its own citizens who put it in power?

Surely if it is the government in the wrong it can't use the Espionage Act on an innocent investigative journalist. But we strongly want to argue that an investigative journalist can use the same principle to trigger the First Amendment Act/Magna Carta Clauses 39 & 40 to hold a government to account that has not just posed a risk to its people but actually caused the deaths of 3000 civilians.

172.   The First Amendment.

173.   *The First Amendment provides that Congress make no law respecting an establishment of religion or prohibiting its free exercise. It protects freedom of speech, the press, assembly, and the right to petition the Government for a redress of grievances.*

174.   Although the U.S. Constitution's First Amendment protects freedom of speech, any speech that poses a "clear and present danger" to the public or government loses this protection.

175.   Likewise, the public under the First Amendment Act has the protection of freedom of speech especially the publications of government secrets where in this case there is a clear and present danger created by the government or its foreign policy that triggers the overriding of the Espionage Act.

176.   Proximity and degree of the Existing, Clear, and Present Danger.

177.   A harmful event triggered by the government that has already caused harm on the country's soil and an event that has not been contained where the public is obligated to override the Espionage Act in the interest of protecting civilians of the same government from further harm.

178.   The basis here is the fact that if a government can curtail freedom of speech to prevent the effects of that speech vis-à-vis the citizens. It follows too that the public, especially journalists and publishers have the right to make void the government's Espionage Act if there is already an

Existing, Clear, and Present danger. The event or danger must satisfy the following criteria for it to suffice and for the journalist or producer to be justified in revealing government secrets relating to the danger.

179.   Proximity.
180.   ..nearness in space, time, or relationship.

181.   For the case to stand scrutiny; the event which is an existing, clear, and present danger must.
182.   a} Have occurred already on the soil of the government concerned.
183.   b] Have a link to the government's acts, foreign policy, etc. There must be enough evidence or hints of links to the government's acts and the event.
184.   c] The degree of harm must be high, and this event has already claimed the lives of innocent civilians and the journalist or publisher can prove that it's a causal-effect relationship between the government's acts or foreign policy with the event. Several people would have died to justify overriding the Espionage Act. Death of innocent civilians must have been witnessed by many people, especially on national television or an event eyewitness can prove happened. The reason is that the journalists and publishers etc. can step in the government's shoes and in reverse say we are overriding the Espionage Act because it is your government that has already put the lives of innocent civilians to harm and as such stop. Let others scrutinize this case before you cause more deaths. Let us open an immediate inquiry to find out if your acts for sure are the ones that have already caused the deaths of civilians.
185.   The Espionage Act is proactive law that gives governments powers to curtail freedom of speech in order to stop and limit the effects of exposing government secrets in the public interest.
186.   Whereas the Existing, Clear, and Present Danger gives journalists, producers, and the public in general rights to curtail the powers of the government where it can be

proved that it was the government that has already caused significant deaths on its own soil and as such everyone is obligated to limit the government's impact in an escalate to de-escalate the situation.

187.   Points to note here are. The harm must have already occurred and have been witnessed with undisputed proof of this.

188.   It can be proved that if no action is taken the risk of the event reoccurring is high and any citizen is obligated to act in order to prevent further harm to civilians.

189.   All this happening and the future risks must have happened and be expected to happen on the government's soil. The case will not suffice if future threats are to occur in another country etc unless the same government is as well responsible for that other country.

190.   Degree.

191.   *the amount, level, or extent to which something happens or is present.*

192.   The event in this situation must be of horrific magnitude to justify overriding the Espionage Act requirement. The idea here is that the government has already triggered one of the worst atrocities in the history of the United States. So, this justifies exposing them in order to control the situation where there is no other way. In which case if the citizen, journalist, or producer does not do anything then the risks of the events happening again on the country's soil are high, and silence or no-action can't be tolerated.

193.   Traumatic inducing effects of the event.

194.   The event must have happened already and must have caused so much trauma that a lot of people have witnessed this and have been affected by this. Traumatic events like the 9/11 event are so distressing that they influence what people would do after witnessing such events. The events would have been so horrific seen or

witnessed by people on national television enough to have an effect.

195. The magnitude and extent of the event.

196. The number of deaths.

197. The event must have happened on the soil of the government.

198. The event has been linked to the government's acts or foreign policy directly or indirectly.

199. The event must have been recorded and has been viewed by many and can be replayed repeatedly over a long period.

200. The area, position and symbolic meaning where this occurs must be considered as well. That is like with the 9/11 event; the Twin Towers were a symbol of American pride as the tallest buildings in the world at the time. The importance and values attached to it are paramount as well because like in the 9/11 case; the destruction of such buildings brings fear into the people's lives that increases the extent of the trauma that is going to be experienced by the people.

201. Three types of trauma to be experienced in such situations.

202. A] Two years of Trauma.

203. Firstly, witnessing such events as 9/11 as it happens has the effect of traumatizing people on a large scale considering this happened on the soil of the government with more than one event and all occurring simultaneously to paralyze the country with fear and panic without giving anyone a chance to do anything about it. This event will temporarily incapacitate everyone who has witnessed it. Rendering all as temporarily unable to make sound decisions due to fear. This will influence how people will behave for the next two

204. years.

205. Yes. This lasted for a good two years when people would react differently due to fear than how they would have reacted if they had not witnessed an event like 9/11.

206.   In this traumatic stage, people due to fear will stick with the government no matter what. Even if they know that it was the government's acts or foreign policy that brought about such evil own its people. Fear of this happening again will make most people not criticize the government. Everyone supports the government unless whatever it wants to do is linked to what caused the event in the first place. After 9/11 even though some criticized the government due to the fear induced by the event, not all supported a war that had a chance of triggering fresh revenge attacks due to the government's foreign policy.

207.   Even if the people have information about the government's evil acts abroad. No one was willing to jeopardize another event like 9/11 at least that soon. The government itself in this stage is fearful and doesn't make harsh decisions. It would suspend its foreign policy for some time or do things underground while the pains and traumas are still fresh. In this stage people put faith in the government; they just go with the flow. They think they have only the government to protect the personal liberties and lives of the people.

208.   Two years after the trauma has passed.

209.   Any traumatic event lasts around two years and after that, the pain fades away and people are no longer incapacitated in that now they can challenge the government. They start making decisions based on facts and rationalizing things. After the trauma has faded. In this stage, they discover that one way to stop this from happening is to head-on address the government as well. In this stage, they see the government as a risk. The government is now the enemy of the people. You can hear people publicly attacking and criticizing the government. They start making decisions based on rationalizing things and not from fear.

210.   Five years and beyond.

211.   In most cases, the government would have embarked on an even full-scale operation of exactly what caused the event in question as a means to deal with the threats in clamping down say terrorists as in 9/11. By 2003 two years after the event when the traumas and fears of the event were fading off the government summoned full scale military operation and invaded Iraq after spending two years bombing Afghanistan. To most people, this triggers a new wave of fear of the 9/11 event happening again. But at the same time now the trauma has faded, and they rationalize everything and discover that the government is the problem.

212.   Unless someone takes the law into their own hands the risks of the terrorist attacking again are increased. This is because the government will intensify the attacks as revenge attacks. Some citizens after remembering the event e.g. 9/11 can vow to do something about this. In order to right a wrong using the Escalate in order to De-escalate method so as to get the government stopped and scrutinized.

213.   This triggers the exposure of government activities that are likely to trigger another event like 9/11. Some people feel obligated naturally to protect civilians by curtailing government acts. Exposing them but not to report them to international courts, no. But so that there is a shift in policy.

214.   Investigative journalists are prominent in this stage. This is due to the heightened risks of the danger and pain being suffered again by the innocent civilians. They might argue that "the government must be stopped before they outsourced terror again on its own people" This stage is characterized by the fact that it has become public knowledge that the government is involved in illegal activity abroad.

215.   It is the government's actions that caused the 9/11 event.

216.   The government will have intensified its operations by now.

217.   But will have not changed what they were accused of by the terrorists, as reasons for the attacks. To some people's surprise and shock the government will be committing even more war crimes abroad.

218.   This triggers some people to notice that the situation has reversed. The government has stepped in the civilian's shoes; one who needs to be controlled by the Espionage Act in order to stop putting lives in danger.

219.   The major difference is that at this stage the Existing, Clear, and Present Danger would have manifested itself. This is because people will have died in numbers. 3000 died in the 9/11 attacks. Yes, the government will be at it again. This means clear and present danger in that by this time also the government will not have got who they regard as the real people behind this.

220.   Osama Bin Laden only got killed in May 2011 after Wikileaks released materials [9/11 pager messages released Nov 2009, April 2010 Iraq possible war crime video, Aug 2010 Afghanistan war logs, end of 2010 CIA files,] all this to escalate the situation in order for a resolution to be achieved.

221.   This is a fact. That means he contained the threat or triggered the government to take the threat seriously. In fact, protecting the American citizens from another 9/11. They waited 9 years to get Laden. It took six months from releasing of the information to the assassination of Laden. Surely only after the release of the material in an escalate to de-escalate. Assange is the unlucky American hero, one who can put the FBI and CIA out of business. Probably the reason why they are after him. Protecting their jobs at his expense nothing to do with national security. But if he is an American hero, why is he in prison?

222.   The fact that the government is still committing war crimes abroad creates panic. It is like asking the government if it is out of its mind because people have already died, and it is still doing the same, yet they haven't even got the masterminders of the attack. It is like what if

they attack again? No way I am going to expose you so that someone stops you.

223.   So, the government will not only have increased the war crimes that triggered 9/11.

224.   They would not have got Osama Bin Laden or even Al-Zawahiri.

225.   So, the risks are still very high. This triggers fears of another surprise attack that in the end one is forced to act in an Escalate to De-escalate.

226.   First, you must understand why Terrorists engage in terrorist acts. This is for two major reasons.

227.   First, Terrorists arise for revenge for what they believe are wrongdoings against their people usually by a foreign power in their own country. The direct intention of their activities is to revenge as a way of equaling the evil act attributed to the government.

228.   Secondly,

229.   The aftermath of their acts which are mainly meant to shock and traumatize the people has another reason; that of triggering the rise of the government's critics in the country they are going to attack. These arise after the two years of the trauma of witnessing the event have passed. I explained above that in the first two years fear and trauma cause people to not react or simply support the government just because they are traumatized enough. To avoid this from happening again. They make decisions based on fear hence the temporarily incapacitated clause.

230.   After two years the trauma and fears will have faded away. Now the people start realizing that the government is the one who caused the event and as such start realizing that if they want to solve the problem, they must address the government. Hold the government accountable. This is not a coincidence but the aim of the terrorists. Terrorist have a one-time chance to revenge and they know that after the revenge there is a 95% chance, they will be dead or be imprisoned for life.

231.   Most believe they have a duty to stand for the defenceless even if that means their deaths. So, they embark on a shock and traumatise act. One that will last for more than two years. So, for this to be possible they make sure that the event.

232.   First, It is so shocking and horrific to be remembered for years.

233.   Secondly, they clearly state their grievances and the reasons why they are carrying out this evil act. 9/11 event; America has been evil to their people in their own country and they are here to translate that evil on American soil.

234.   Thirdly, They clearly point out who is the problem. It is your government because it doesn't care about you. So, remove them. This is because if they cared about their own people they would have not gone to the terrorists' country and killed women and children knowing that the terrorists will come to America to revenge. This is only done by a government that doesn't have the interest of its people at heart. One that is outsourcing terror and evil to its own people. As such must not be trusted to govern as they are acting against the people who put them in power.

235.   Over the years especially after the two years have elapsed the people use this as a stencil to check and scrutinize its government.

236.   Fate as well means the government will not change. Such an attack actually gives the government the right to do whatever they want. They now go for women and children of the terrorist as revenge but also to show power.

237.   This naturally triggers investigative journalists who upon witnessing events like 9/11 now becomes cautious and proactive in preventing another 9/11. For most this is enhanced by the fact they would have felt helpless and guilty for not doing something to stop this from happening in the first place. That sixth sense would tell them to be alert and do what is right. After all, it is the government that is outsourcing harm. So, who is going to stand for the women and children who are caught up in all this? Who stands for the defenceless? This triggers the need to act since the government can't help. 'Publishing evidence' in

an Escalate to De-escalate is now the only option. In order to hold the government publicly accountable for their actions.

238.   This triggers the need to expose evil. Only with the aim to safeguard the lives of the people in public interest but viewed as a direct challenge to government power.

239.   Hence the strictness of the government in this case which is as good as putting the king on trial and having him beheaded. Ever heard about King Charles I of England?

240.   In other words, the journalist's investigative acts of releasing the information and the publisher's acts is an indirect declaration that.

241.   i] The government is out of control and as such must be controlled. Who needs a renegade government?

242.   ii]It can be proved that the state with its reckless foreign policy has abused the secrecy powers in a profoundly undemocratic way that if not scrutinized will only bring more pain to the people.

243.   In short, the terrorists themselves indirectly put in a place [through this horrific act] a system that triggers the rise of independent investigators who will be critiques of the government. These journalists and producers of the materials are important to the existence of a near-democratic system.

244.   Journalists unlike the often-misunderstood notion that they bring or put lives in danger. Actually, acts as vital checks and balances of a near-perfect democratic process. Especially where a government is causing the deaths of its people on its own soil. That alone triggers the need for independent investigative journalists with powers to report the government abroad if it fails to cooperate.

245.   This also proves that the Espionage Act violates the First Amendment Act.

246.   The Espionage Act applies the men's rea standards that does not consider the public interest defence. But it can be argued that since it's the government at fault and one that has already caused the deaths of its own people and made things worse on its own soil. This means that every citizen has the right to hold the government to account and

make them answerable. Hence why most governments would apply the same harsh punishment as that in treason cases.

247.   Treason and dealing with the charges of.

248.   ***Treason*** *is the crime of attacking a state authority to which one owes allegiance. [1] This typically includes acts such as participating in a war against one's native country, attempting to overthrow its government, spying on its military, its diplomats, or its secret services for a hostile and foreign power, or attempting to kill its head of state. A person who commits treason is known in law as a **traitor**. [2]*

249.   Wikipedia

250.   The government considers indirectly the Espionage Acts as a mild form of treason to some extent in that they try to accumulate charges so that they match the same fate as one being tried for treason.

251.   Not saying that is correct but it's the government's way of stamping on government critics. The hard treatment also points to the guilty part of the government where the material is released and published as they regard it as unauthorized.

252.   This has the effect of removing the people's ability to hold the government to account.

253.   D] Escalate to De-escalate.

254.   You must note that where it's a citizen who tries to bring future risks of harm to the people. The government uses the control apparatus to contain the effect of such exposure. In this case, the government is proactive. It is there to stop and prevent the effects of exposing government secrets before harm falls on the people.

255.   The case in which it's the government's acts that are bringing harm to the people then citizens are obliged to act. They aim to expose the government. To escalate the situation. Once exposed the government must contain the

issue by reducing or controlling further war crime abuses. This brings in other players. Critics of the government denounce it so that it takes a different route.

256.   Here the idea is not to report the government to an outside institution like the international courts but a genuine need for the government to be scrutinized so that it changes its events to stop further deaths or future risks.

257.   Releases and publications are meant to reveal only proof of what is already public knowledge. Anything released at this stage is not new information. This is because the Existing, Clear, and Present danger would have made the accusations public information. After 9/11; tapes and other information revealed that the terrorist attacked the US citing the US's foreign policy as the trigger. War crimes of previous wars etc. In most cases, the government doesn't take a strong stance in refuting the accusations but does not admit to such acts happening either. Any investigations etc are faced with stalling tactics.

258.   It is important to note here that the releases and publications of information are meant only to act as proof. Once again there is no new information at this stage. Everything released is public knowledge but without proof. For example, WikiLeaks's video release in 2010 was not new material. Everyone knew there were accusations of war crimes.

259.   The aim of the journalists and producers of the information is to rally critics to denounce the government so that it changes its policy in a protective way.

260.   The situation here makes it a strong case to justify overriding the Espionage Act.

261.   This is because.

262.   a] The informational release is targeted at the government itself. The journalist and publishers release the information for the government. Yes, no matter how weird it sounds. The target for the information is the government itself.

263.   That means the Espionage Act is irrelevant here. This is because this information is sent back to the rightful

people in the government who make changing decisions that affect change. Not to enemies of the government.

264.   Espionage.

265.   *"the practice of spying or of using <u>spies</u>, typically by governments to obtain political and military information. [intended for another government typically foreign.]"*

266.   Government's accountability. The rights of citizens to hold the government to account.

267.   Clearly, this can't be regarded as an espionage act because the information is intended for your own government and they might say 'we all know what you did last summer. Change your acts, put your house in order or they are going to come again. We know too that it was you [the government] who caused the deaths of all those people. So, change now before they strike again.

268.   All this is the right of citizens to hold their government to account.

269.   Lack of mentioning of public interest in relation to the Espionage Act.

270.   The Espionage Act does not offer a public interest defence because it is applicable only on two occasions. This Espionage Act only acknowledges Investigative journalists and spies on one end and those who think they can challenge the government. The journalist and producers of the materials. But the current laws and thinking suppress automatically those who want to hold their government to account as in government accountability and the citizen's right to hold them to account.

271.   This right is there in law, but governments want the view that they are above the law hence no citizen has the right to criticize them or hold them to account.

272.   But this right is a universal right, but you must satisfy the above conditions as well as the following for this to hold water.

273.   Your acts are not an intention to take the government to court. There are no threats of getting the government punished etc here. This is because if threatened the government will enable its defensive and protective mood and attack.

274.   We believe this is the case with Julian Assange. The government thought he wanted to take them to court for war crimes. So, in a protective way of their soldiers they mounted a relentless attack on the Wikileaks founder.

275.   Mind you 9/11 attacks [especially being caught off guard and their slow reactions] will have activated the government to act fast and crack down on anyone they think is a threat. The effects of the 9/11 attack would have rendered them useless in the eyes of the people who would have witnessed people dying without anyone trying to help as they were unable to do anything. Now they want to make up for the humiliation suffered then and improve their public image and credibility as well. All this by attacking first as a defensive approach. Suffering the loss of 3000 people would make the death of a reporter unimportant to them. Especially one they already regard as an enemy of the state; surely would make no difference to them.

276.   The casualties suffered already make them disregard all laws and rules and might just imprison anyone they want just to show power.

277.   Surprisingly the true intention of the release of classified documents and their publications is to protect the people from the harm the government is outsourcing through its foreign policy. Deep down all are only interested in correcting a wrong. Even though monetary gains can be assigned to such acts it's the sheer realization that a citizen can have power [To hold the government to account through citizen rights] but mostly to save people from further harm. Although these people can be regarded as big-headed to think they can do better than the government, their actions are in the public interest. To

actually expose a corrupt and reckless government that outsources terror and keeps doing the same at the expense of the people. This makes the people take the law into their own hands.

278.	This is critical as it also explains why the Espionage Act does not give the option to use the public interest as a defence because these are not acting in the interest of the public but in the interest of their own firstly.

279.	DOES THAT MAKE SENSE?

280.	Another way to charge the people with TREASON.

281.	These people even though not stated in the acts are regarded as involved in treason as they are trying to remove the government. The government knows they are not acting in the public interest as such even though they are but are challenging the government by discrediting it.

282.	This is the reason why they are very strict with such cases and would aim for maximum sentences because in truth they would have already killed the government the very moment they released proof that the government is terminated since it caused the death of the people who elected it.

283.	But this is how America through the Thirteen colonies was founded. This is how your constitution was written. This is how you come about with a Bill of Rights. In theory, Julian Assange and Manning are the same as your founding fathers. Julian Assange is George Washington, Thomas Jefferson, Benjamin Franklin, John Kay, Alexander Hamilton, James Madison, John Adams, and Abraham Lincoln.

284.	The major reason why this case is different from other cases under the Espionage Act is the fact that in all other cases the government is in control [it is innocent as it did not bring harm to its own people] in that it can be acting to actually protect the public. Any act it takes from now on is to prevent perceived or real harm to civilians. But in this case, the government has outsourced terror through its foreign policy and the terrorist did not hesitate and attacked killing 3000 people. Automatically the government stopped existing as it can be proved that it is the one responsible for getting 3000 people killed through a reckless foreign policy. Julian Assange by publishing the material has judged the government and found it unworthy to stand for the people and must cease to do so.

285.   But the government is corrupt instead of amending its acts will forever relentlessly pursue Assange as now technically he has more power than it has. He has already dissolved it.

286.   Hence through a crackdown, the government will aim for maximum sentences.

287.   First Amendment act.

288.   But the first Amendment act gives rights to individuals to express themselves and powers to scrutinize the government and hold it accountable since no one is above the law. This Act also gives rights to individuals to assess serious government abuse of its people on its soil that would otherwise continue without accountability.

289.   Gives citizens the right to monitor and check for egregious abuses of the law.

290.   The Acts act to contain assaults by the government on the freedom of the press.

291.   These Acts stress the importance to know more about any serious acts by the government that amounts to abuse.

292.   This Act also gives rights to the protection of the security, identity, and safety of those who leak information.

293.   Above all this gives protection and rights to investigative journalists.

294.   Even though the Espionage Act does not give citizens the right to use the public interest defence it gives them more power to hold the government to account on the basis that everyone is equal under the law and that citizens have the right to hold a government accountable.

295.   Existing, Clear and Present Danger.

296.   We know the defence of public interest vis-à-vis the Espionage Act on its own won't succeed but why worry when we can use the Existing, Clear, and Present Danger defence to hold the government to account?

297.   I explained above that the government even though they will not mention it will use or equal treason laws in disguise against a person charged as such.

298.   Consider themselves as having rights to hold you indefinitely even without charges as exactly what is happening in the Assange case.

299.   The government will group a bunch of charges that amount to the same sentence as that of treason. Are you surprised the US compiled charges that have the potential to get Assange imprisoned for up to 175 years?

300.   That means only a president or king can pardon the subject.

301.   The person to contact would be the president, prime minister or king, etc. One who might exercise his rights and pardon the subject. A direct approach to one of these as the courts are unlikely to deal with these issues as they will simply enforce these.

302.   Counter.

303.   The judge might rely on the Espionage act to declare that.

304.   ..there was unauthorized possession of access to, control over,.. information relating to national security to willingly communicate, deliver transit ... the same to any person not entitled to receive it.

305.   "The Act will require the government to prove that the defendant had reason to believe the information could be used to the injury of the US or to the advantage of any foreign nation."

306.   As a citizen a person who put the government in power in the first place, is entitled to hold the government to account where there is evidence that it is the government that is bringing harm to its people. As a citizen, he is just

exercising his rights to highlight the issues the government must address.

307.   The information is directed at the government and there is no proof that the subjects' acts are directed at the courts but directly at the government so you address the pressing issues and all this [even though not explicitly stated] is the need to prevent further deaths.

308.   The fact that the country suffered horrendous terror attacks that in itself is reason enough to trigger the right to scrutinize the government making them aware of a potential issue that must be addressed as a matter of urgency.

309.   Further in defence the "Existing, Clear and Present Danger" in the form of 9/11 attacks removed or makes the "unauthorized possession, distribution, access to control over... information relating to national security to willingly communicate, deliver transit ...the same to any person not entitled to receive it.." null and void.

310.   The First Amendment Act gives any individual where the Existing, Clear, and Present Danger exists; the right to hold the government accountable. So, questioning why you accessed information etc is void. [an evil has been done and the civilian is acting as the replacement authority to hold the government to account]. The fact that the government breached its trust is a risk to the lives of Americans and this null and voids the unauthorized notion.

311.   The existence of a criminal act attributed to the government shifts the focus of journalists and publishers to make them independent inquiry civilians endorsed by the First Amendment Act to scrutinize the government where people have died and where there is documented proof.

312.   The right of the government that requires it to " prove that the defendant had reason to believe that the information could be used to the injury of the US or the advantage of a foreign nation" cease to exist where it is the one [the government] outsourcing terror that has brought pains and sorrow on American people.

313.   If the government is the one that caused the deaths of its own citizens, then the roles change. The citizen now

stops being a journalist or publisher but becomes the advocate of the right of the dead-victims, a judge, or an investigator who goes on to collect evidence to assess the extent of the guilty part of the government.

314.   This means if people have died the government being involved ceases to have any rights to question or hold a citizen at ransom.

315.   The last resort is to do what the Act expects you to do, that is to; "behead the corrupt government" "through a counter as a bargaining tool so that the government drops charges as well as you. Draft a court case of not just putting people in danger but using the Existing, Clear, and Present Danger notion that the government can be said to have contributed to the deaths of the people in such acts.

316.   Existing.

317.   3000 Americans died in the 9/11 attacks.

318.   The previous government and foreign policy are to blame. Their war crimes abroad have triggered revenge attacks.

319.   These revenge acts have happened on American soil meaning the government can longer represent the people nor is it in a position to protect them. Remind it that it's the people who put it in power. Outsourcing of terror actually resulted in deaths.

320.   Clear.

321.   Now we have proof that the government even now has not changed its acts and is still doing what triggered the 9/11 attacks this renders it incompetent and unable to represent the will of the people as it keeps doing what might still bring more harm. Russia and Ukraine war. Check our Perfect Russia and Ukraine War Prediction.

322.   https://play.google.com/store/books/details/David_ Gomadza_A_Perfect_Prediction_Russia_Ukraine?id=Pma VEAAAQBAJ&gl=GB

323.   Foreign invasion and war crimes increase the risks of another attack putting even more lives at risk.

324.   Present Danger.

325.   The danger is even heightened in that the terrorists who the government says are responsible for masterminding this are still at large.

326.   So, you make a case against the head of the government, the president, the minister, etc.

327.   Declare sudden death. Like cowboys ask to a gunfight.

328.   Walk away from each other count ten steps turn and whoever shot first wins.

329.   Sudden death.

330.   Or since there is a counter. If you drop any charges against him, I will drop all against you as well.

331.   Background Material.

332.   According to the Amnesty International petition.

333.   The US charges allege that Assange conspired with Chelsea Manning to illegally obtain classified information. They want him to stand trial on charges under the Espionage Act and the Computer Fraud and Abuse Act in the US where he could face a prison sentence of up to 175 years

334.   .

335.   The US government's indictment poses a grave threat to press freedom both in the United States and abroad. The conduct it describes includes professional activities undertaken by investigative journalists and publishers on a daily basis. If Julian Assange's extradition is allowed, it would criminalize common journalistic practices and permit the US, and possibly other countries, to target publishers and journalists outside their jurisdictions for exposing government wrongdoing.

336. *The US extradition request is based on charges directly related to the publication of leaked classified documents as part of Julian Assange's work with WikiLeaks.*

337. *Publishing information that is in the public interest is a cornerstone of media freedom and the public's right to information about government wrongdoing. Publishing information in the public interest is protected under international human rights law and should not be criminalized.*

338. *If extradited to the US, Julian Assange could face trial on charges under the Espionage Act and under the Computer Fraud and Abuse Act. He would also face a real risk of serious human rights violations due to detention conditions that could amount to torture or other ill-treatment - including prolonged solitary confinement. Julian Assange is the first publisher to face charges under the Espionage Act.*

339. *Julian Assange is currently being held at Belmarsh, a high-security prison in the UK, on the basis of a US extradition request on charges that stem directly from the publication of disclosed documents as part of his work with Wikileaks.*

340. *Julian Assange's charges according to Amnesty International relate to his publishing activities as part of his work with Wikileaks.*

341. *Julian Assange published documents that point to the US's possible war crimes committed by the US military between 2003 to 2008.*

342. *The US's relentless pursuit of Julian Assange is seen as a full-scale assault on the right to freedom of expression.*

343.   *According to Amnesty International Julian Assange if extradited*

344.   *to the US, he faces a real risk of serious human rights violations including possible detention conditions that would amount to torture and other ill-treatment (such as prolonged solitary confinement). The fact that he was the target of a negative publicity campaign by US officials at the highest levels undermines his right to be presumed innocent and puts him at risk of an unfair trial.*

345.   The pursuit of Julian Assange is considered a full-scale assault on the right to freedom of expression.

346.   *The fact that he was the target of a negative publicity campaign by US officials at the highest levels undermines his right to be presumed innocent and puts him at risk of an unfair trial.*

347.   *The US authorities must drop the charges against Julian Assange that stem solely from his publishing activities with Wikileaks.*

348.   This disingenuous appeal should be denied, the charges should be dropped, and Julian Assange should be released' - Agnès Callamard Amnesty International.

349.   *Amnesty International calls on the US government to drop the charges against him and the UK government not to extradite him but release him immediately.*

350.   *Yahoo News revealed that US security services considered kidnapping or killing Julian Assange when he was resident in the Ecuadorian embassy in London.*

351.   *There are reports that the CIA considered kidnapping or killing Assange and these have cast even more doubt on the reliability of US promises and further expose the political motivation behind this case.*

352.　　"It is a damning indictment that nearly twenty years on, virtually no one responsible for alleged US war crimes committed in the course of the Afghanistan and Iraq wars has been held accountable, let alone prosecuted, and yet a publisher who exposed such crimes is potentially facing a lifetime in jail.

353.　　"The US government's unrelenting pursuit of Julian Assange makes it clear that this prosecution is a punitive measure, but the case involves concerns which go far beyond the fate of one man and put media freedom and freedom of expression in peril.

354.　"Journalists and publishers are of vital importance in scrutinizing governments, exposing their misdeeds, and holding perpetrators of human rights violations to account. This disingenuous appeal should be denied, the charges should be dropped, and Julian Assange should be released."

355.　　https://www.amnesty.org.uk/press-releases/usuk-julian-assanges-politically-motivated-extradition-must-not-go-ahead?utm_source=google&utm_medium=grant&utm_campaign=&utm_content=amnesty%20international%20julian%20assange&gclid=CjwKCAiAs8acBhA1EiwAgRFdw0W00CEKRoFrnybTCtGEODdQIB4lVZ-aoR9rgl89trIIOzCAffEH2BoCiQ0QAvD_BwE

356.   FREE JULIAN ASSANGE

357.   Tomorrow's World Order's Perspective.

358.   David Gomadza

359.   The effect of personal liberties in the establishment of the United States' Constitution.

360.   American founding fathers were inspired by the doctrines of personal liberties enforced by the Magna Carta. For Benjamin Franklin and Thomas Jefferson, personal liberties and freedom of speech were seen as the natural rights of a man, especially against an unjust and reckless [oppressive] government.

361.   Magna Carta. Clause 39 & 40.

362.   *"No free man shall be seized, imprisoned, dispossessed, outlawed, exiled or ruined in any way, nor in any way proceeded against, except by the lawful judgement of his peers and the law of the land.*

363.   *"To no one, will we sell, to no one will we deny or delay right or justice."*

364.   *UK parliament laws. Magna Carta.*

365.   To the founding fathers, it was the context in which personal liberties were exercised or denied. It was the presence of a cruel and [unjust] or reckless government that gave more significance to its power over personal liberties.

366.   So, the context here is more important in that where a government is so cruel or reckless enough to endanger the lives of its citizens. On top of that it breaches all personal rights of the people and then goes on to suppress their freedom of speech and other liberties then this issue becomes of paramount importance.

367.   The question that needs to be answered here to ascertain whether the publishing of the material released is a breach; is whether the government can be regarded as just and protecting the people's liberties or reckless enough

thereby putting the lives of the American people at risk itself.

368.   There are cases in which the release of the material acts as a means to protect US citizens. The question we need to answer here is the fact that has the government's acts contributed to the risks that the country suffered in the past before the release of materials? That makes the exposure of such information trigger a change in government policy which in turn would help to protect even more; the American citizens.

369.   Escalate to De-escalate.

370.   We as Tomorrow's World Order can argue that Wikileaks leader Julian Assange might have actually acted in a way that exposed the bad practices in order for the government to correct their bad acts to avoid future harm to the American citizens in an escalation to de-escalate.

371.   We need to assess the situation leading to the war and the trigger of the war, the events in the video released, and the situation during the time of the release of the material.

372.   Had the USA suffered evil beyond human comprehension before the events in question?

373.   I argued in my books [pen name: Carolinadeivid]; The Vice President the Electronic Transfer Volume I & II Volume II

374.   https://img1.wsimg.com/blobby/go/e8972857-57d8-43db-80d4-9913437629c9/downloads/The%20Vice%20President%20The%20Electonic%20Transfer%20Volu.pdf?ver=1669509863615

375.   That the idea behind 9/11 was to traumatise people in a shock and instil fear now. Not just for a few years but for decades to come in that the terrorist or the master-minder knew that the effects would be recorded and broadcast to the public live. What a coincidence for the first plane to hit just when camera crews were under the towers rehearsing something else.

376.   Nevertheless, the master minder wanted to instil the greatest fear in the eyes-witnesses' lives and everyone else who will see the live broadcasting. This; so as to trigger an uprising against the government's foreign policy as a way to de-escalate the situation. Same tactics as those used by the West of imposing sanctions that kill women and children so as to trigger the uprising of the opposition to the government. People who will defend the innocent victims by fighting or exposing the government.

377.   In the east, it is believed that a reckless government that goes on to kill others abroad no matter for whatever reason doesn't really care about its own people. Most terrorists would argue that such a government must be removed by its own people simply put because their actions or foreign policy is to blame for the evil befalling its people.

378.   Caring for its citizens means having a good foreign policy abroad. Reckless behaviour can only bring pain and doom upon its own citizens. To the terrorists, they aim to trigger a local uprising that will expose the government's reckless behaviour so as to trigger actions that lead to change.

379.   This was the intended effect of triggering an uprising that will fight or expose the government but in such a way so as to stop any further escalations. This is evidenced by the fact that terrorists are revengeful and therefore reactive in that they all attack after something has happened first. Look at all major terrorist events; the terrorist cites past wrongdoings as the triggers of such acts. Look at 9//11 in the USA look at July 7 bombings in the UK, look at the beheading of the British soldier in Woolworth. There is a pattern. The attacks are meant to trigger local revolts that fight the government in such a way as to stop the reckless evil acts or behaviour in the first place.

380.   So, I reiterate that 9/11 was just meant to do just that. Scare people to death so they stand up to the government's foreign policy in an escalate to de-escalate. The terror attacks on live television were meant to instil

fear that will remove the fear of the government. Instil fear that people would stand up to their own government so as to stop further attacks of this kind.

381.   I elaborate here that the 9/11's acts were meant to instil immediate fear so as to shock and scare the people in a revengeful way. This fear as we all know has a life span of two years. Any traumatic event would last roughly two years influencing a person's acts, attitudes, and behaviours. After two years have elapsed the body tends to forget or place less emphasis on the events as compared to the first two years.

382.   The second part of the 9/11 terrorist acts was to trigger and continuously influence the lasting fear of such events occurring that will trigger citizens into action. For the first two years after the event, most people would not take action or dare even criticise the government even if they know or knew that the terrorist act was a direct result of the government's reckless foreign policy. The trauma of witnessing such events live or on national television would render most incapable of rationalising the events. It is meant to render all incapacitated in that fear of death would make them side at first with the government. Who by this time would be actively publicly denouncing the acts even if they know that the act was a direct response to their foreign policy?

383.   The main effect of the terror act is that of triggering uprisings. This would start taking effect after the immediate act of shocking and incapacitating the eyewitnesses starts wearing off. As I said after two years. People, after the elapse of two years would act as if they have woken up from a trance. The effects of shocking them and rendering them incapacitated would have worn off or started to do so that now they will start thinking rationally and logically.

384.   I can argue that the first two years after the event are characterised by less criticism of the government. People's fears make them think irrationally in that even if they know that the government was responsible for the events that triggered the terror attack. They would still support the government or not oppose it at all. To make

things worse even if they know that the government is about to repeat the same reckless foreign policy act that triggered the attacks in the first place. The shock, fear and scare effects of the terrorist act render them incapacitated or unable to rationalise this. In normal circumstances, citizens would voice concerns and can clash with the government in that they can fight the government citing why would they repeat the acts that brought this doom in the first place.

385.   But the attributes of the terror event render the people temporarily incapable of sound judgement or rationalising the situation.

386.   The manner in which the events occur.

387.   a] There must be some rehearsal of a similar event at the very same time or near the time of the event. This gives people a sense of relaxation. Picture a group of news crews with cameras at the same time of the event; rehearsing how they might tackle a terrorist event. Picture the army rehearsing war games at the same time. Picture July 7 London bombings a private company linked or not linked to the government rehearsing a terror event at the same time the terror happened. Coincidence or not the intended effect is to take the people from one emotional continuum to the other, from a relaxed mood where some might even rub off the event as a rehearsal but only to discover that the event was real. The second effect is for this to be absorbed slowly by the brain so that it lasts for a long time. Events that occur out of the blue can quickly be absorbed and understood that they might not have lasting effects even if they were shocking. Now picture an event that for some time no one knew was real or not. The confusion and the shock and the feeling of being unable to respond quickly as you would say where there is no confusion about whether it was a real event or part of the rehearsal. The blame on oneself for taking things lightly and the feelings of being caught unguard bring the guilt and confusion that will make the brain keep bringing all this up

so that a person thinks about this for a long time. But the effect of all this is to trigger a change in response in that after the two years have passed; the citizens go into a pro-active mood in that they become on guard and alert after that. The fear that had rendered them temporarily unable to make sound judgement would have worn off and the fear of the event occurring again will now act as a trigger for them to act as the citizens would have acted within the two years.

388.　　　Now after two years most citizens would be willing to fight even the government with the aim to stop the repeat of the terrorist events. Now the aim is to never see that happen and to reduce civilian casualties even if that means acting against the government. The event is so traumatic in that it cannot be justified now to rely on Espionage Act reasons.

389.　　　Especially now that the government itself is the one that brought the terror event itself through its foreign policy. Some citizens would work on their fears and calculate the risks of being targeted by a reckless corrupt government vis-a-vis the risks of protecting American citizens. Now some might see a huge opportunity to do what is right and protect the American people from further suffering. Wishes for the government to lose elections, the presence of a strong opposition party all would trigger others actually exposing the government. First in the hope that the exposure would contribute to their downfall. After all, they are the ones who triggered the deaths of 3000 citizens. An opportunity to set the record straight and do what is right since if the system was right the government is the one who ought to be dragged to court for a reckless foreign policy that resulted in the deaths of its citizens.

390.　　　So, the looming elections after the two-year period would justify others acting as investigative journalists. So as to correct a wrong. This is a right of every citizen where the government is no angel, a corrupt reckless government that is putting the lives of 3000 American lives at risk. The nature of the terrorist event, their said beliefs and reasons for the attack, and the number of deaths all will act to ascertain the weight to be relied to in justify this argument.

391.   No doubt 9/11 was probably the worst terrorist attack on American soil. The most shocking of all. That brings me to the second point.

392.   b] The event must render everyone useless-to-help to have a lasting effect. I explained in my book The Vice President the Electronic Transfer Volume II the Death Trap [links above] that 9/11 was so sophisticated that it involved a lot of people other than the 'cave-men' terrorists. Whoever masterminded 9/11 knew how to create a death-trap and the knowledge required some inside information. The angle at which the plane hit the building and the position where it hit the building was meant to create a death trap.

393.   One that would block the only means of exit so that everyone inside would be trapped in such a way that even if there were a thousand ways to be helped out of the towers exiting was rendered impossible. The planes destroyed the lift and stairs system to trap everyone inside. So, the event was to render everyone useless to enhance their fears. Imagine mighty America with the best military; actually, training at that time therefore ready but unable to do anything or save anyone. Imagine probably the best firefighters unable to do anything. The main effect was to make people not react by being made hopeless. Imagine people jumping from the 100th floor to their deaths. Imagine fires and smoke raging and with no one to do anything. The helicopters rendered useless as well as everyone. Imagine everyone just watching on national television unable to save the people. Imagine firefighters fighting to their own deaths? But the real effect is the cries and calls for help where people were told to sit and wait. Just because there was nothing else anyone could do. The calls for help that never materialised and the witnessing of the deaths. Especially where they are told to sit and wait until the time the towers collapsed on them has the effects of triggering the need to act after the shock and trauma period of two years has warned off.

394.   This is critical in this case because this will trigger later in years to come the need to act and not just sit. The need to act fast as well. The need to do what is right and act upon it no matter what.

395.   Secondly, the event and helplessness of the people and the way they died with no one even the government unable to act would trigger the need to do something and the sheer recognition that the government is unable to do anything when expected. Picture the president at the time shocked and sitting unable to do anything for some time. Picture the people on the buttress columns not just waiting for help but actually making the last decisions on how they are going to die. Either burn in the fire, get choked to death by the smoke, or jump. All this with no one to help or do anything beneficially. Now picture the firefighters dying themselves trying to save the people.

396.   Now picture a person who has witnessed all this discovering proof that it was all along the truth that it is the reckless government's foreign policy behind all this and the fact that despite the event they are still doing even worse than what was allegedly in the first place. Surely given the conditions of 9/11 above it is reasonable that a person can act as an investigative journalist in an escalate-to-de-escalate situation. All in the hope of stopping the repeat of 9/11.

397.   Now here is where my arguments override all the accusations. Chelsea Manning was trusted, vetted and authorised to access government material. She knew the rules and regulations. She was aware of the Espionage Act. But after 9/11 it can be argued that the fears of such events occurring again and the need to correct a wrong become paramount to an extent to override the fears of being targeted or persecuted by the government under the Espionage Act. We argue that if it wasn't for 9/11 then the government would have been justified to use the Espionage Act etc against these. But where the government is at fault then this chasing and persecution becomes void and illegal under our laws.

398.　　　It can be argued that the release of the footage did not bring new knowledge or expose new information. After 9/11 it had become common knowledge that the government was doing something wrong and had done something wrong through its foreign acts. No one needs proof of what the government did. 9/11 was enough event to cast doubt on the innocence of the government.

399.　　　Secondly, every war is followed by an investigation of war crimes, etc. So, we argue that the exposure of the documents was not material as this was public knowledge already by the time of publication.

400.　　　Thirdly if it wasn't for these the courts would have requested such materials or called a witness to point to events that occurred during the war. Since there are patterns, where foreign soldiers in self-defence etc end up killing civilians etc. Also, the fact that another third party [Reuters] had requested the same material through legal means would have highlighted what had happened with the release or not.

401.　　　The materials only made it vivid rather than as publication of new information that was not there in the first place.

402.　　　We strongly believe that even if the so-called investigative journalists did not intend to do that. They acted [just as a post 9/11 intended act that of now acting] as safeguards of peace both to the terrorists' people and to the American people. I argued above that after two years had elapsed the trauma would have varnished. People in this state of being temporarily incapacitated to make sound judgements now they are invigorated and acting as safeguards to peace just as the terrorists' original intention that of triggering local uprisings to challenge the government.

403.　　　It is a fact that terrorists view a reckless government with a bad foreign policy as not caring for its people. They go on acts like this to stop all this from happening. They rejuvenate the locals and offer them reasons to stand up for what is right. This is the aim of terrorist acts. To revenge and install critics of the government because from the word go it is the government that needs changing. Since terrorists are reactive in a revengeful manner, they are not able to guarantee that the events won't happen again. But to do that they create situations that trigger the rise of government critics who will challenge the government in a manner that creates a change in foreign policy and the ruling government itself.

404.　　No matter how it might sound. All this in order to protect the American people. Most terrorists know they are given only one chance. The very reason why they will always look for permanent solutions to the problems is by triggering the rise of government critics who will do whatever it takes to avoid future conflicts. Simply because most terrorists know that they have only one shot at revenge and that their missions are suicidal. They don't expect to live after the event.

405.　　This is critical to the case. We as Tomorrow's World Order argue that this situation will always create people who will go one step ahead of all this in order to safeguard the lives of the American people. The fact that the events can fall under war crimes gives the government justifications for chasing after the investigative journalists so as to cover their acts. The situation and fact that this can be considered a war crime make the government become stubborn and persecute these just to protect its soldiers. No court or journalist will pursue the issue as long as the government is chasing these. This can be a distraction of justice.

406.　　First-hand liability of the government to its own civilians' deaths.

407.　　The Espionage Act might not apply where a government is itself making actions that are causing the deaths of its own people. It can't justify protecting a few soldiers at the expense of 3000 American citizens. Where a government's acts are putting the lives of its own people on its own soil in danger this makes the Espionage Act irrelevant here even in Chelsea Manning's case. The fact that the events occurred on American soil means that the government is not in a position to protect its own people on its own soil and this incapacitates it. Any citizen can act so as to protect the American people by denouncing or exposing the government.

408.   If the events had happened abroad then a different situation might have been reached.

409.   The time frame it took them to resolve the issues that triggered the 9/11 event is critical also here.

410.   The fact that the government could not find Osama until 02 May 2011 [only after the release of documents that helped pinpoint the whereabouts of Osman based on the evidence in the released pagers message the day of the event. Documents released in November 2009] in itself justifies any release of the documents. Especially the discovery that the government was still doing what caused the 9/11 event.

411.   It is open to me to conclude that the failure of the government to resolve the Osama Bin Laden issue until 02 May 2011 strengthens the case that even if it wasn't intentional. The exposure actually protected the American people in two ways.

412.   It lessened the determination of the terrorists to keep avenging as one of their goals was fulfilled that of triggering uprisings among the locals who will stand up to the government. They had achieved that and hoped for regime change within the USA so as to stop foreign abuses while at the same time lessening the need to mobilise terrorists to mobilise. The exposure meant government scrutiny not just by the opposition party but by international systems and courts.

413.   The fact that Bin Laden who the government believed was the man behind all this was at large and the risks that he could mobilise another attack justified internal changes as well. If the government can't contain the threat of Osama Bin Laden, then it must lessen the effects of its foreign policy so as not to trigger revenge attacks. So, the exposure at such a critical time might actually have prevented further deaths of the American people. In that,

the government reduced its foreign policy's impact abroad so as not to attract revenge attacks. In this case, document release might have actually prevented further attacks on American soil.

414.   Another critical point is the fact that the exposure of American soldiers' acts abroad considering the fact that their target number one was still at large actually acted indirectly to make the government contain the threat by making them more determined to deal with the issue. Which they did by 02 May 2011.

415.   i] The investigative journalists can be credited with pushing the government to deal with the terrorist leaders so as to prevent further attacks on American soil. So, exposing the information render the government exposed in that they had to act immediately and go after Osama Bin Laden.

416.   ii] If it was not because of the exposure of the documents in 2010 the government through the FBI and CIA might have remained complacent to the dangers posed by Osama Bin Laden and taken their time.

417.   It can be argued that they only acted adamantly after they were rendered useless through the exposure of their secrets. This is what mobilised them to act fearing that now the terrorists might know their acts. If it wasn't for this then up to now some of the terrorists could still be alive.

418.   iii] We believe Wikileaks gave the FBI and CIA leads on how to get hold of Osama Bin Laden all the FBI and CIA had to do was to go through the 500 000 pager messages released by Wikileaks in November 2009 and trace anyone linked to Osama Bin Laden.

419.   Wikileaks publishes 570000 messages capturing chaos of 9/11

420.   https://www.theguardian.com › media › nov › wikileak...

421.   25 Nov 2009 — **Wikileaks** publishes 570,000 messages capturing chaos of **9/11** ... The mental and emotional storm that struck America on 11 September 2001 with the ...

422.   Mind you for 9 years they had no leads of where to find him. Good 9 years and just after one year of Wikileaks releasing documents they got their man. Wikileaks exposed their methods as a way to tell them that if they are insisting on using their sophisticated digital methods, they will never get Osama. Leave all this fanciful technology and go back to basics. Tract the pager messages.' Few months they got Osama. Check how they got him? Not through sophisticated drones etc; no. He was using a pager. The information Wikileaks released in November 2009.

423.   The FBI and CIA worry about their jobs, not that Assange was a threat.

424.   To add to the above point is the fact that it took the government twenty years to deal with Osama Bin Laden's right-hand man, whom the current president only ordered to be killed this year in august. The killing of Ayman Al-Zawahiri took twenty years. The exposure could have softened the terrorists or given them a false sense of security that the international world would act, and that America would change its foreign policy. All this could actually have prevented further trauma for the American people, especially on their soil.

425.   The fact that it took the government twenty years to deal with Al-Qaeda with the killing of Ayman Al-Zawahiri [Osama's right-wing man] means that the exposure had no material effect. If this had exposed the government to the risk of putting lives at risk, then it would not have taken the government twenty years to deal with this threat.

426.   Surely it is open to me to argue that if that were true the government would have intensified its acts and crackdown on AlQaeda, especially with the footage of Osama Bin Laden with Al-Zawahiri the man who took

over. All this points to the fact that the exposure actually helped the government in covering their war crimes and shifting the blame to the investigative journalists. Assange protected the American soldiers otherwise you all could have waited until they had gathered enough information. Assange acted this way as a damage control. Up to now twenty years on no court can touch your boys and girls. This alone means all charges must be dropped.

427.   It can be argued that the government went after Manning and is now going after Assange as a deterrent to those thinking of going after its soldiers for war crimes. It worked. Your boys and girls are free twenty years on. It's time for him to taste freedom again.

428.   What are you afraid of?

429.   The government is protecting itself from itself by being determined to get Assange. The timeline of events can reveal that major events or dealings with the effects of 9/11 only occurred after the exposure and publication. This as I argued above could contribute to resolving the issues and thereby actually protecting the American people. The exposure removed the complacency and made the FBI and CIA propose a plan that helped them get Osama Bin Laden.

430.   We need to assess what the international community and the courts say about the government's war crimes. I argued above that the publications did not expose new material. 9/11 hinted at a bad foreign policy. Surely no one will target a country to such an extent as they did the USA without being wronged or feeling that way even if that was not the intended aim. 9/11 was meant to destroy the fabric of the American people. Had United 93 not crashed who knows what might have happened? If the courts looked at the issues in exposed files, then it can be argued that it is not material who exposed and published the materials. Little weight should be paid to this.

431.   The fact that no major incident happened to America on American soil can help explain that the exposure of the material was not material but actually

invigorated the government to pursue not the investigative journalists but the terrorists themselves.

432.   The fact that the terrorists were alive even up to August this year meant that the government did not recognise itself; the exposure and publications were a material fact so as to the threat of such publications. Surely if that was the case, giving the terrorists more reasons to repeat 9/11 the government would have intensified its crackdown soon after release so as not to give the terrorists opportunities. The material publication actually helped the government decide better what's best for Americans.

433.   It is open to me to argue that there is no evidence that either Manning or Assange did this for monetary gains. In this case, their priorities and intentions whether implied or expressed could be brought into question as to their real motives. Again, I reiterate that it does not matter whether they intentionally planned to help prevent further attacks on the American people or not. The fact that the timeline of events below suggests that their acts acted to actually invigorate the government to act on the still-at-large threat actually helped secure the lives of the American people.

434.   Involvement of a Third Party. The British government covering their acts to look good and blame the USA for everything.

435.   British issues at hand that could have contributed or worsened the situation at hand.

436.   i] Britain had falsified dossiers used to justify the war. They wanted information to justify the war. A genuine excuse. So huge incentives to encourage leaks of information they can use to claim that they had foresight that leaked documents would put people in danger. It wont change a thing when the documents were leaked. They had to contain the situation as previous wars had already created war crimes.

437.   ii] Huge World War II debt they owed the US.

438.   iii] Deep financial issues.

439.   iv] Political issues locally needed a boost.

440.   v] Long fuel queues at the pump and high fuel prices after Saddam reduced production of oil.

441.   vi] Squatters at Chagos who were refusing to go after Britain evicted them.

442.   vii] America's taking the spot of the global leader from Britain.

443.   One other line of thought I want to highlight is the fact that the two Manning and Assange might have been set up in a trap so as to clear the other player in all this; The British Government but exonerating it of any wrongdoings at the expense of the Americans.

444.   The two facts I will look at here are the following. First is to establish the links between the USA and the British government.

445.   Secondly, establishing the links between the British government and Manning.

446.   Thirdly, establish the links between the British government and Assange.

447.   Another line of thought as I mentioned above is the fact that the British government and not Assange as argued by the Americans are the ones who helped Manning to get the documents and get them published. The aim being to clear the British of any wrongdoing and any war crime accusations at the same time smearing the USA.

448.   First of all, I want to point to the fact that we as Tomorrow's World Order have discovered that somehow the British go back in time to the 1660s and recreate events so as to replay these using the script then. All this is to gain the favourable advantage of knowing exactly what will happen next.

449.   We used the 1665–1667 Anglo-Dutch War script after suspecting that the British are fighting a proxy war in the Russia and Ukraine war. Read our book first or soon after to check the accuracy of our prediction. We published the book with an ISBN that is dated so you check the accuracy with what is happening in the Russia and Ukraine war. The truth will shock you.

450.   https://play.google.com/store/books/details/David_
Gomadza_A_Perfect_Prediction_Russia_Ukraine?id=Pma
VEAAAQBAJ&gl=GB

451.   It is a fact that Manning was associated with
Pembrokeshire. So, if a third party was involved then we
can only infer from evidence of places lived that since
Manning grew up in Pembrokeshire. The British consider
Wales their country and the Earl of Pembrokeshire is
regarded as one of the "best knights that ever lived" even
though he lived as far back as 1189. The British document
everything. If the theory is correct, we believe that
Manning was groomed as a knight but not any knight but
the well-known knight in Pembrokeshire folktales, William
Marshal, The Earl of Pembroke.

452.   *Knighted in 1166, he spent his younger years as a
knight errant and a successful tournament competitor;
Stephen Langton eulogised him as the "best knight that
ever lived."[3] In 1189, he became the de facto earl of
Pembroke through his marriage to Isabel de Clare, though
the title of earl was not officially granted until 1199 during
the second creation of the Pembroke earldom. In 1216, he
was appointed protector for the nine-year-old Henry III,
and regent of the kingdom.*

453.   Wikipedia.

454.   *...When King Stephen besieged Newbury Castle in
1152, according to William's biographer, he used the
young William as a hostage to ensure that John kept his
promise to surrender the castle. John, however, used the
time allotted to reinforce the castle and to alert Matilda's
forces. When Stephen ordered John to surrender
immediately, threatening that William would be hanged,
John replied that he should go ahead saying, "I still have
the hammer and the anvil with which to forge still more
and better sons!" Subsequently, a pretence was made to
launch William from a pierrière (a type of trebuchet)*

towards the castle. Stephen could not bring himself to harm young William. [6] William remained a crown hostage for many months and was released following the peace resulting from the terms agreed at Winchester on 6 November 1153, by which the civil war was ended.

455.   Wikipedia.

456.   *First, before we get deeper, we need to look at the life of William Marshal Earl of Pembroke which might paint a picture about the young Manning. If any.*

457.   *Knight- Errant.*

458.   *As a younger son of a minor nobleman, William had no lands or fortune to inherit and had to make his own way in life. Around the age of twelve, when his father's career was faltering, he was sent to the Château de Tancarville in Normandy to be brought up in the household of William de Tancarville, a great magnate and cousin of young William's mother. Here he began his training as a knight. This would have included biblical stories, Latin prayers, and exposure to French romance literature to confer precepts of chivalry upon the future knight. [7] In Tancarville's household he is also likely to have learned practical lessons in the politics of courtly life. According to his thirteenth-century biography, L'Histoire de Guillaume le Marechal, Marshal had enemies at Tancarville's court who plotted against him — presumably, men threatened by his close relationship with the magnate. [8] ....*

459.   *In 1166 he was knighted on a campaign in Upper Normandy, then being invaded from Flanders. His first experience in battle received mixed reviews. According to L'Histoire, everyone who witnessed the young knight in combat agreed that he had acquitted himself well. However, as medieval historian David Crouch remarks, "War in the twelfth century was not fought wholly for honour. Profit was there to be made..." [9] In this regard Marshal was not so successful, as he was unable to translate his combat victories into profit from either ransom or seized booty. L'Histoire relates that the Earl of Essex, expecting the customary tribute from his valorous knight after the battle, jokingly remarked: "Oh? But*

Marshal, what are you saying? You had forty or sixty of them — yet you refuse me so small a thing!" [10]

460. [Emphasis added]

461. *In 1167, he was sponsored by William de Tancarville in his first tournament, where he found his true calling and began to develop skills that later made him a tournament champion.*

462. *In 1168 he served in the household of his mother's brother, Patrick, Earl of Salisbury. Later that year Patrick was escorting Queen Eleanor on a journey near the boundary of her province of Aquitaine and Marshal was part of the escort. They were ambushed by Guy de Lusignan who was trying to capture Queen Eleanor, Patrick was killed but Queen Eleanor escaped. In the ambush, William received a wound to his thigh and was taken to a Lusignan castle to be held for ransom. Someone at the castle took pity on the young knight because it is said that he received a loaf of bread in which were concealed several lengths of clean linen bandages with which to dress his wounds. This act of kindness by an unknown person perhaps saved Marshal's life as infection of the wound could have killed him. After a period of time, he was ransomed by Eleanor of Aquitaine, who was apparently impressed by tales of his bravery. He would remain a member of Queen Eleanor's household for the next two years, taking part in tournaments and increasing his reputation as a chivalrous knight. [11]*

463. *.... Marshal followed the Young King, and from 1176–1182 both Marshal and the Young King gained prestige from winning tournaments. [13] Tournaments were dangerous, often deadly, staged battles in which money and valuable prizes were to be won by capturing and ransoming opponents, their horses and armour. Marshal became a legendary tournament champion: on his deathbed, he recalled besting 500 knights during his tournament career. [14][15]*

464. [Emphasis added].

465. *Wikipedia.*

466.	But the most important point why I looked at this William Marshal Earl of Pembroke is the *fact that he served King John the King well known for the Magna Carta.*

467.	*…… Despite their differences, William remained loyal throughout the hostilities between John and his barons which culminated on 15 June 1215 at Runnymede with the sealing of Magna Carta.*

468.	[Emphasis added]

469.	Wikipedia William Marshal Earl of Pembrokeshire.

470.	I opened this judgement document on Julian Assange/Manning versus the USA by mentioning that, I quote.

471.	*American founding fathers were inspired by the doctrines of personal liberties enforced by the Magna Carta. For Benjamin Franklin and Thomas Jefferson, personal liberties and freedom of speech were seen as the natural rights of a man, especially against an unjust and oppressive government.*

472.	*To the founding fathers, it was the context in which personal liberties were exercised or denied. It was the presence of a cruel and unjust government that gave more significance to personal liberties.*

473.	Ladies and gentlemen, what is this Magna Carta?

474.	Wikipedia describes it as the great Charter of freedoms. The very charter used by the founding fathers to fight for independence especially against a cruel oppressive reckless government at the time. First, what freedoms are guaranteed by this charter and the relevance to the case at hand?

475.	*Magna Carta (also Magna Charta; "Great Charter"), [a] is a royal charter [4][5] of rights agreed to by King John of England at Runnymede, near Windsor, on 15 June 1215.*

476.	*……First drafted by the Archbishop of Canterbury, Cardinal Stephen Langton, to make peace between the unpopular king and a group of rebel barons, it promised the protection of church rights, protection for the barons*

*from illegal imprisonment, access to swift justice, and
limitations on feudal payments to the Crown, to be
implemented through a council of 25 barons. Neither side
stood behind their commitments, and the charter was
annulled by Pope Innocent III, leading to the First Barons'
War.*

477.   *At the end of the 16th century, there was an upsurge
in interest in Magna Carta. Lawyers and historians at the
time believed that there was an ancient English
constitution, going back to the days of the Anglo-Saxons,
that protected individual English freedoms. They argued
that the Norman invasion of 1066 had overthrown these
rights, and that Magna Carta had been a popular attempt
to restore them, making the charter an essential foundation
for the contemporary powers of Parliament and legal
principles such as habeas corpus.*

478.   *.... Jurists such as Sir Edward Coke used Magna
Carta extensively in the early 17th century, arguing against
the divine right of kings. Both James I and his son Charles
I attempted to suppress the discussion of Magna Carta. The
political myth of Magna Carta and its protection of ancient
personal liberties persisted after the Glorious Revolution of
1688 until well into the 19th century. It influenced the early
American colonists in the Thirteen Colonies and the
formation of the United States Constitution, which became
the supreme law of the land in the new republic of the
United States.*

479.   This is why I went back as far as 1189 so that you
understand that whatever is happening is happening for a
reason. The Magna Carta was widely used to challenge
kings who believed in the divine rights of kings. Kings who
trampled personal liberties. Kings who put the lives of the
people at risk. Kings who imprisoned people for a long
time without charges or redress. Kings who thought were
above the law. Kings who disregard what is right but who
crackdown on freedom of speech. Above all reckless
corrupt kings. If our working hypothesis is correct, the

British at the time in question and the Americans believed that the government which was endorsed by a king was above the law.

480.	In that, they engaged in a foreign policy that brought harm to the people themselves and used out-of-touch laws to suppress freedom of speech and other personal liberties. Throughout this legal document, I have argued that there are certain cases where the acts of a government are the ones bringing harm to the people. In such cases, all citizens are obligated to act so as to escalate in order to de-escalate thereby actually preventing any harm to the lives of the people. In such cases, Investigative journalists are actually acting in the interest of the citizens rather than putting the lives of the people at risk as the government wants you to believe.

481.	In such cases how can you strike the balance between national security and the protection of citizens and the protection of personal liberties? Is imprisonment without charges like in the Assange case justified especially considering the length of time held in a high-security prison for expressing one's personal liberties and where there is evidence that the previous government's acts through its foreign policy have contributed to horrific acts like the 9/11?

482.	Would such imprisonment not amount to a breach of personal liberties, especially where even if not expressed the publications actually protected the lives of the American people? Would this not amount to excessive powers of the government? If no one can hold them answerable for their acts does this give them the right to go after investigative journalists who act in the public interest and national security? Can all this, especially after the time held in prison be justified or is it time for the government to swallow their stubbornness and free these people? Thank them and compensate them?

483.	I opened this case with food for thought that if the so-called investigative journalists were that wrong it follows that the founding fathers were wrong too and as such I will point out later. The British can argue that they leased the thirteen colonies [USA] to the forefathers see the case of Chagos below. Or that they were wrong to use the Magna Carta to establish the constitution of the US. It can be argued that it was not just defending personal liberties per se that enabled the establishment of the USA but the presence of a corrupt government that oppresses and brings harm to its people. Therefore, acting against citizens because there is a clear link between the harm that befallen the people and their foreign policy.

484.   I argued that if it wasn't for the 9/11 attacks then the government could be justified that the publications brought harm to the people. But surely after being traumatised by 9/11 events any citizen or foreigner automatically inherits the obligation to act. During 9/11 the government did not act. No one acted and all witnessed everyone perish. Surely finding out [even if the information was public knowledge] that the government is at it again would trigger any human being around the world to act. Especially the fact that the leaders of AlQaeda were still at large. This can be regarded as a scream for help on discovering a fire. Surely it is human nature to scream for help in order to contain the situation.

485.   It can't be argued that the publication of such material was intended to trigger more terrorist acts even if Assange is not American by birth. Magna Carta then and personal liberties give every person on earth the right to act to protect humanity at large.

486.   It can be argued that some countries are so closed that they swear on sticking together as one through pledges of allegiances. Meaning never challenging the government even if it is the one bringing harm to its own people. It is like an abusive husband. Just for safety and protection and a roof over her head the wife even if being abused might keep silent and not report any wrongdoing. But is this right? If the wife had a chance to report the husband without the fear of being victimised would the wife report the abusive husband?

487.   We argued that if it wasn't for these the courts or Reuters could have gotten the material anywhere over time. Having said that the government must assess who else could have requested the material published and would they have released the material by now.

488.   We saw President Trump releasing the assassination of JFK files after a certain period no matter what this meant for national security. So, we have precedence. It can be argued that by now this material could have been officially released by the government to Reuters, pressure groups, or international courts.

489.   So again, it is not justified to keep holding these and as such they must be released, and compensation awarded.

490.   Assange and Manning are no different from the founding fathers who used the importance of personal freedoms over the right of governments to imprison the people who challenged them using the Espionage Act where the government is at fault and has caused the deaths of not ten or hundred but three thousand people. Surely such acts especially considering that the terrorist leaders were still at large at the time of writing. All this calls for the immediate release and dropping of all charges against them and the redress through compensation schemes and a change in government policy and dealings with personal liberties.

491.   *Magna Carta still forms an important symbol of liberty today, often cited by politicians and campaigners, and is held in great respect by the British and American legal communities, Lord Denning describing it as "the greatest constitutional document of all times — the foundation of the freedom of the individual against the arbitrary authority of the despot".*

492.   Wikipedia.

493.   We would like to believe that this was a missed opportunity to put new laws that reflect modern times. Surely, we can't throw away hard-earned personal liberties

just because terrorists decide to attack and cause harm. After all, terrorists are reactive meaning revengeful so would not attack first unless wronged. Meaning that if we are serious about addressing all this some laws like the Espionage Act might not apply considering the past events that put the lives of the American people at risk. Secondly where the government is outsourcing terror to its own people directly or indirectly. Such situations need a look at this from all angles hence the establishment of Tomorrow's World Order. A New World Order.

494.   A closer look at Manning.

495.   Firstly I would like to point out that Four clauses of the original 1215 Magna Carta (1 (part), 13, 39, and 40) remain in force in England and Wales (as clauses 1, 9, and 29 of the 1297 statute).

496.   It can be said that Manning moved in 2001 to Haverfordshire, a place in Wales Pembroke-shire. I linked above the relevance of this city to the forks or history of William Marshal and his link to King John who signed the Magna Carta in 1215 as a way for peace. The basis on which the American constitution was based.

497.   It can be inferred also that since the above sections of the Magna Carta are still in force in England and Wales therefore, she strongly believes in correcting a wrong by doing a right. Having gone to school in Wales it can be argued that she was taught to do what is right. She was taught about personal liberties. The rights of individuals to feel obligated to do what is right despite the rights of the government. So even now she might still not see your point of view that you think she was in the wrong. Simply because no government is above the law. This is the world we all believe in hence the rise of Tomorrow's World Order. A world where if a government outsourced terror and harm that befalls its own people then they must be brought to judgement. I believe that too as I explained above if the government is the one that is responsible for the deaths of 3000 people.

498.   It can be argued that she was trained directly or indirectly as a knight during the time she moved there knowingly or not. The British do that. I lived in Britain for some years, so I am aware of their customs etc.

499.   Personal Liberties Vs Pledge of Allegiance.

500.   We believe the issue here has nothing to do with what is right or wrong. We strongly believe that the government here is targeting these simply because they are not the so-called Americans. I said this because the USA insists on the pledge of allegiance just as the British. A pledge to fortify your rights as a citizen especially in condemning the government. A pledge not to oppose the government even if that means them abusing you too. I can argue that those who don't oppose the government are not being abused themselves. Surely if the government is treating you right even if they abuse others why would you care? Tough luck as long as I have peace.

501.   But what if the government is abusing you as well? Using all tricks, they do to you to commit war crimes. To commit an abuse of personal liberties where they chip all kids and foreigners at birth. Then through advanced drone technology and electromagnetic nerve tampering remotely pass electric currents through your genitals all your life simply because how can you report such acts without being considered as hallucinating? Picture being tortured every single day nevertheless remotely. Picture all government officials; people in a position of power using all banned illegal methods to secure their jobs.

502.   Picture all depending on evil hacking for jobs, where the doctors and hospitals torture people to breaking point with electric diodes fired into the body at birth and miniature plane parts. All drone technology digitally hoods you so that vision is lost so that you get into an accident. Or ambushed by a person they have sent with a GPS chip where they set up police officers to shoot innocent unarmed people, so they have jobs.

503.   Now picture where the chips are implanted at birth and over years foreigners who are religious are then tricked into believing that they are given messages through dreams by God or Allah. But in fact, the chipping at birth is used to replay recorded voices of the subject. That when the person's own voice is used, and messages replayed deep in the inner ears to emulate the inner voice. The brain upon recognising the voice will convert the messages played deep in the ear to dreams. As in hypnosis. The person who is deep in sleep might think he or she received the messages from Allah, therefore, thinking that he or she was dreaming. But can Allah or God tell people to go and kill others? Are these real dreams or the work of very clever digitally advanced corrupt governments?

504.   Now imagine where the government steals your work, steals your information and twitches your body remotely through a diode you can feel. Imagine knowing that they are using a video sender or receiver to check all your work. Hacking your phone, your computer, etc and after years of studying them you find out that they are nothing more than just crooks. The whole system is built on abuse. All jobs of people in a position of authority are created through the abuse of personal liberties. Hacking at birth, remote nerve tampering, hacking to damage otherwise healthy organs, torture and everything that strips away personal liberties.

505.   They even practise secret slavery where they use chips, and diodes are used to replace the whip with a zap of electricity. Picture inserted [miniature] dog collars in all foreigners or all kids. Surely knowing that all this is happening to you. When you expose them, they pretend it's them teaching you. But can someone tell you something that brings their own destruction. Surely can a rotten corrupt government tell you that they are secretly hacking everyone now and torturing you? Now imagine them admitting killing foreigners using the chips and actually torturing you. Then ask you not to tell or expose them when they are doing the same to you so meaning killing you

softly as well. Is it human nature to keep quiet if they are putting everyone on death row from birth simply because you are a foreigner?

506.   Again, I stress out that Americans like the British rely on 'Pledges of Allegiance' to guarantee that no one will report them. But then again if they are abusing you as well would you keep quiet? I can argue that anyone with other roots other than full American will have problems in America.

507.   It can therefore be argued that.

508.   a] The area if outside the USA can influence the person's perception of what is right or wrong.

509.   b] Someone born outside the USA and is not full American can be treated differently just because they are not full American. The demands on the Pledge of allegiance is the only thing stopping others from complaining. This is the reason why the government is having issues with Assange. If they were Americans, they would not have criticised the government even if the government goes on to get 3000 people killed. Please.

510.   But I have highlighted above that the only reason why Americans don't voice against the government is the simple fact that they made the pledge of allegiance to stand by the president rotten or not. Again, you can't expect the same treatment between Full Americans and Australia-born Americans. So, government laws can be said to be discriminatory and prohibit everyone to voice their concerns. The pledge of allegiance has silenced everyone from saying bad things about the government. Just as the fact that Assange was born in Australia so outright not trusted and someone whom the government will crack down on no matter what. Even if he intended to actually protect the American people.

511.   If they can pardon Manning who leaked the documents in the first place, they can pardon Assange. Unless if they don't know that he was in and is still in British jail for them.

512.   [I think Britain has something to hide too.]

513.   Please note that I am not apportioning blame or comparing the two. No, I am arguing that the system, in this case, looks biased towards non-full Americans as such all charges must be dropped considering the time Assange was held in prison by their counterpart war ally in Britain on false account. As such, we demand the immediate release of Assange before Christmas without any charges. Tell the British to release him.

514.   We believe that the pledge of allegiance is the only reason why full Americans can't challenge the government. That is yours and theirs rights. But Assange was taught to stand up for justice. It's not a crime. See life from other's angles as well.

515.   *"I pledge allegiance to the Flag of the United States of America, and to the Republic for which it stands, one nation under God, indivisible, with liberty and justice for all."*

516.   Manning is full American, born in Oklahoma. Yes, that is true but could simply be regarded as not patriotic enough after having been educated in Wales since 2001 if the Wikipedia post is correct. Here it can be inferred that Manning might not feel as belonging to the United States. Probably his treatment in the army might have triggered feelings of not belonging. Secondly, like I argued above, parts of the Magna Carta is still in force in England and Wales. The historic importance of Pembrokeshire where he lived and was educated and the association with the Magna Carta could have given him/her another view of the world. Views so strong that no one is above the law. Views that a government that causes the deaths of its people must be held accountable, pledges of allegiance or not.

517.   Thirdly the British might have influenced her beliefs to such an extent that she chose to have pledges of allegiance not to the American President but to the King or Queen. After all, she is only doing what the founding fathers did. The very reason why we have the United States and its constitution. If this is wrong, then the British are

justified in saying they only leased the thirteen colonies to the Americans on a long lease just as they did in the Chagos case. Where they possessed the Chagossians and leased the land to the Americans making them accessories as well so that in the end instead of standing for justice they would side with their ally in Britain.

518.　　　Manning is entitled to argue that if standing up against a corrupt government outsourcing terror and death of its own people whether full Americans or not was wrong then it follows too that the founding fathers were wrong. The British instead of giving them freedom imprisoned them. Can Britain claim later on that they leased the USA to the Americans on a long lease?

519.　　　Chagos saga and the terrorist attacks of 9/11.

520.　　　The British expelled the Chagossians from the Chagos Archipelago just before 9/11 and leased the land to the USA to establish their base. It is a fact that the British tricked the Chagossians by removing them by small boats and giving them hope that they would return only to ban them with no means of return. But just before 9/11 there were reports of some 'squatters' refusing to leave.

521.　　　The twisted ankle saga.

522.　　　If you look at the map of the Chagos island and the flight paths of 9/11 it is a match. A map of Chagos.

523.　　　We believe that if we are correct then the idea was to establish interrogation facilities at Chagos as a way to deal with the squatters. The Chagossians who were refusing to go away.

524.　　　Mind you this was a steady income for Britain leasing the land to the US for 50 years.

525.　　　Every reason to safeguard the investment.

526.　　　Before 9/11 some squatters often caused problems with the security company. The Chagossians were refusing to go. But after 9/11 with the establishment of interrogation facilities, the attitudes of the squatters.

527.　　　So, it can be argued that if it wasn't for 9/11 then no interrogation facilities would have been established here especially considering the fact the British had lost in court even though the judgement was advisory. They had limited powers to remove the squatters. Only 9/11 made things possible.

528.   We have pointed out also that the British can in the future claim that just as they have leased the Chagos to the USA they leased the USA states of, New York, Pennsylvania, Washington, Boston, and Philadelphia to the USA see the 9/11 flight paths.

529.   Back to the analysis of Manning in all this.

530.   Manning could simply have chosen to only pledge allegiances if he/she thought the government was doing the correct thing.

531.   According to Wikipedia a biography by Nicks September 23 2010; As a child, Manning was opinionated about the intersection of religion and politics.[42] For example, she invariably remained silent during the part of the Pledge of Allegiance that makes reference to God.

532.   Or our other opinion is that she might have felt affiliated with the Queen rather than the president of the USA. That brings us to the possibility of the British having a part in all this.

533.   The British through the secret training to be a knight-errant might have promised her a better life than she had. As a knight, she would end up wealthy. After all, the tournament games and the training empathised with the need to make profits either through ransom or sale of possessed items.

534.   This being just an inference one can argue that yes, the US government was right that someone could have tricked Manning to do what he/she did. Just using allegiance to the Queen as a cover-up. As I said Pembrokeshire was known for being the brave and best knight in William Marshal. The British as heavily involved in all this could have promised Manning protection. Or used allegiance to the queen's oaths or simply acted his or her need to make a wrong right to clean their army and country. So that only the USA can be implicated in war crimes etc.

535.   It is a fact the British government made up dossiers that were used to justify the invasion of Iraq. It only came out after the war that they managed to repay the Second World War debt they owed the USA a day after Saddam Hussein was hanged. They could have used the release of material to throw the focus off themselves and smear the USA in all this at the same time clearing themselves of any wrongdoings.

536.   It can be argued that all the 9/11 plane hijackers were all known to the officials. It can be started that it could be the truth that some terrorist were complaining that the West are killing ethnics using miniature versions of plane parts [drone technology] with GPS properties to trace, a black box for recording and playback of sounds. This to enable them to manipulate digital hypnosis to trick the terrorist as if they were having dreams from Allah to go and kill others. When in fact it was them.

537.   First Britain was in serious debt, with political and economic woes at home. High fuel prices have meant high inflation. The huge WWII debt they owe the USA and the threat posed by the Chagossians squatters all needed a strategic plan that would resolve all this.

538.   Saddam had reduced oil production after the sanctions.

539.   The Chagossians having refused to be evicted from the land they considered theirs.

540.   Huge debt and political chaos all this might have made Britain be involved in 9/11 hiding behind the terrorist whom they commanded.

541.   implanted chips at birth and then go on to torture the terrorists to breaking points as a rolling of anger approach. Where the terrorist know exactly that it is the British who are remotely torturing them in broad daylight simply because no one can prove it. Then torture them so that they go and revenge this triggering 9/11.

542.   Christopher Wren, a British scientist after the 1665–1667 war and fire designed plans to rebuild the city of London and offered these to the king when London was

still burning. The very plans the King's brother James I The Duke of York [the one whom New York was named after] used to build London's twin sister New York. The same Christopher Wren who designed the buttress and column designs that went on to be used for the building of World Trade Centre buildings.

543.   The very man who devised the Colony Collapse Syndrome after experimenting with bees. Where he designed a glass see-through of the design, the version that was used to design the twin towers with buttress columns and see-through glassed columns. The man who discovered that if bees are trapped and smoke, if introduced, they will run to the top instead of trying to find a way down. In the end they die inside even if there were spaces to escape downward. The same person through introducing the colony collapse syndrome discovered back in the 1660s that if the alpha male is removed and caged in see-through enclosures. The left males will stop feeding or looking for food and if the alpha is kept away the colony will collapse.

544.   The very same scientist who first introduced the idea of injecting substances in the blood and experimenting on people. The very scientist who after the fire he offered to rebuild St Paul's church after the king refused to let him rebuild the city. Do you know he was the first to use gunpowder to destroy the leftover columns of the church after the fire? In his experiments, he used gunpowder to destroy the remaining walls of the church. He used 3 kg of gunpowder to lift 3000 kg of rubble. Does that sound familiar? Do you know how many people died in the 9/11 attacks?

545.   Do you know plane fuel and aluminium if mixed can produce the effect of gunpowder? The same man who refused to pay compensation or was against that when he proposed to rebuild the city of London after the Great Fire of 1666. He realised that traditional methods of destruction then which meant using a huge rod was time-consuming and costly. Faced with the bad condition of the buildings and the pandemic of 1665 that was attributed to dirty and crowded living conditions. He was determined to rebuild

the city. His map of London during the fire of 1666 is the very plan used to build New York where the terrorist event happened.

546.   The very same man who incorporated the idea of time balls in city designs. Where a free-falling ball would be placed on top of the building and a pulley system be incorporated in the design at the basement where a person would simply go down and pull a lever so that the time-ball would drop down. The free fall time was then used to tell the time to help ship captains whose clocks often lost time at sea. This method would tell the correct time. The very principle was incorporated in the design of the Third World Trade centre tower. The controversial tower that free fell on 9/11 against all odds and scientific standards. The very method of the time-ball where the building was built so that when the levers that support the build-on construction are pulled then the building would simply collapse just as it did on 9/11.

547.   Above all this is the very man behind the cycloid, a market prediction tool that uses the time ball to predict the fall of markets. Just as it was used during the time-ball era but now to predict the fall of financial markets. Third World Trade centre free fell for 6,6 seconds in this method meant to mean years. Calculate from September 2001 plus 6 years and 6 months. You get May 2008. Check the exact time of the 2008 financial collapse of the markets.

548.   The very man who had roles with the London stock exchange where they invested buying government bonds etc and selling to make a profit. Check who benefited the most from the financial collapse. Check which banks or financial institutions were in all world trade centres and where their headquarters were. Who bought the financial securities and related products just before the collapse?

549.   The very man whose colony collapse strategy was used in the Guantanamo cages with open or glass enclosures to psychologically immobilise critics into action. Giving the impression that the caged terrorist and others were not ill-treated simply because all this was done in public. Where everyone could see. Going back to his

experiments with bees he observed that even if there was an escape route; bees once they have seen the smoke will go up to the top of the container.

550.   The man who designed the twin towers building or whose ideas were used by whoever designed the twin towers. The angle at which the planes hit the building was a calculated cold-blood plan to seal exits and watch everyone die with no escape or hope of being rescued. The very man who was against compensation for land acquired preferring to have the people experimented on.

551.   The very man against the flamboyant city traders who he observed as not paying enough taxes to make it possible to maintain the city. Not enough taxes were paid by the very rich. Mind you this is just after the 1665 pandemic. He was a religious person as well as interested in churches.

552.   The man who rebuilt St Paul's cathedral. So, the man familiar with the Sodom and Gomorrah incident where God destroyed the evil traders in the cities who oppressed the poor and were involved in insider trading. Do you know how God destroyed Sodom and Gomorrah? Through sulphur and fire from the skies. Can you see a plane loaded with jet fuel as a means of destruction? Aluminium used for aeroplane building mixed with plane fuel produces thermite which is similar to sulphur.

553.   Do you still think it is just a coincidence?

554.   What is the name of the FBI chief at the time in question? Christopher Wren? No, Christopher Wray. Okay, maybe just a coincidence. Do you know what Christopher Wren looked like? A twin photo of Larry Silverstone. But who is Larry Silverstone? The very owner of the World Trade Centre. The very buildings he bought after they were issues with running these. The new standards banning asbestos in buildings. The huge expense of destroying the buildings. His blame of city traders housed in these buildings who insisted on paying the minimum rents, rates, and fees. What triggered the 1665–1667 problems in London? The rats [mice] caused the pandemic contributing to the poor living standards as crowding increased. The

refusal of the riches to pay according to how they earned. Meaning lower standards and a lack of funds to maintain the buildings. What about in New York 2001. High demolition fees, huge maintenance costs, and the city elites' refusal to pay more rates {not rats] for the offices they occupied. The only way to clean the rats is through fire. Just like the evil merchants of Sodom and Gomorrah. Only sulphur and fire from the skies can teach these a lesson.

555.　　　We have Larry Silverstone [carbon copy of Christopher Wren; google search their images. Twins.] getting insurance for the building and inflating the value of these just before the 9/11 events and running to collect the insurance pay-out.

556.　　　Did you remember the controversial video of him saying he ordered to 'pull' down the Third world centre building? Can you recall all the scientists who questioned the free fall of the Third World Centre? Can you recall what I said about the time-ball, the plans used to build New York and the Three World Trade centre buildings? Can you recall the experimentation with gunpowder to demotion building? The Sodom and Gomorrah story?

557.　　　After 9/11 we have the FBI holding people captive for years without trial etc. Recall what I said about William Marshal who advocated for the Magna Carta. This man even though he was religious he was commissioned by the King to be his surveyor for the city of London. The king who believed in the divine right of kings. Enough to do whatever he can; knowing that the king would come to the rescue. Recall the calls to go after AlQaeda and then Saddam Hussein because of weapons of mass destruction. Do you know that they actually used the 9/11 event to implant weapons of mass destruction into all foreigners at birth without consent? The use of drone technology in the form of miniature aeroplane parts and electromagnetic remote-operated nerve tampering. Starting a colony collapse syndrome where the breadwinner males are removed and caged in Guantanamo so that the threats of terrorism' are reduced. Whose ideas again? Christopher Wren's; so, coincidence? I don't think so.

558.   A coldly calculated murder plan. We know that Christopher Wren died a long time ago so who is behind this? Guess? The hospital, government and the police the whole system is just not right. It needs a massive cleanup. They have documented everything and now they collect information through these digital recordings in the disguise of medical records. So far 90% of all people in developed countries are chipped. The government knows everything you did to your wife in private last night. It can tell you how many times she orgasms. How many times did she fake the whole thing?

559.   They are so advanced now they can over the years record all movements and your reaction in order to predict your likely reactions. Now it is possible to turn thoughts into words or audio. So that one can simply listen to all your thoughts. Now they just spy on your activities, interfere in your life, and make it look like they are clever. They can predict what you are going to do. They are simply stealing your designs, ideas, etc, and selling them to the highest bidder. If you notice and complain then use the chips to put radiation through you. After all, who is to believe you?

560.   9/11

561.   The Wikileaks released material started way after 9/11 and as such Wikileaks could have released the material to remind us why 9/11 occurred in the first place. It can be argued that only after knowing about what happened to the USA on 9/11 surely having found such information Julian Assange felt obligated to release the material to trigger change within the American government and how they deal with others.

562.   It is open to me to argue that because 9/11 was probably the worst terrorist act in the history of America and as such anyone would be obliged to become an investigative journalist to escalate and demand change so as to de-escalate thereby actually protecting the American people.

563.   My argument is that the release of the video opens the subject to debate. If nothing had been released the

soldiers could have kept killing people abroad which could have triggered even worse terrorists attack on American soil or Americans abroad.

564.   It is open to me as well to say it is arguable that the exposure had triggered better dealings in war abroad during the Iraq invasion. Now knowing that if they committed war crimes in Iraq, they were bound to be exposed through Wikileaks, this might have resulted in reduced war crimes after the release, therefore actually protecting Americans.

565.   The release might have triggered confessions by American soldiers who would have remained quiet and even worse repeated.

566.   9/11 as a support for the release of materials.

567.   It can be argued that witnessing 9/11 could have justified the release of materials as a way to avoid another repeat, especially because the terrorists themselves attributed the 9/11 attacks to war crimes and killings of other people abroad by American soldiers. One can argue that Wikileaks released the material as a way to get the government into action. Also to the government's opposition party or groups to put pressure on the government to avoid a repeat of 9/11.

568.   It is a fact America suffered the worst terrorist attacks way before the release of the materials. Wikileaks exercised its rights to force the government to take measures to avoid the repeat of the same events therefore actually protecting Americans.

569.   If it wasn't for 9/11 then the release of the material might have been viewed with suspicion. But 9/11 justifies any acts by citizens that correct an unjust and oppressive government, the one bringing harm to the people.

570.   9/11 shifted the blame from the journalist to the government. Wikileaks can argue that it is the government's acts that are bringing harm to the people. Wikileaks can satisfactorily argue that the threat to Americans' peace and safety is the government and not the journalist in that the government through previous wars and invasions has brought the 9/11 attacks. So, it is the government's foreign policy that is getting people killed

and after witnessing 9/11 surely anyone knowing the cause of 9/11 would be obliged to expose the unjust and risk-taking government to force the government to change.

571.   Dealing with an unjust oppressive greedy government.

572.   Can the government be regarded as just and caring for the American people? Can the government be regarded as just doing everything to protect American lives at the time? Surely Wikileaks could have known through their sources that it is the government's foreign policy that is bringing harm to Americans in the form of terrorist attacks. 9/11 itself is solid proof that even if the government was innocent surely something was wrong. 9/11 is proof of a calculated cold-blooded attack with several incidences that the terrorists had murdered the Americans only written all over it. It is the most solid proof of revenge attacks known in recent decades.

573.   Revolution and need for change.

574.   A system failure can trigger the need for drastic measures. Surely you can't expect everyone to act according to the government laws when the government itself is corrupt, oppressive and itself being the master of doom on its people. In some cases, the government might not know or anticipate the effects of its actions, so the responsibility falls on citizens to revolt and escalate to de-escalate and demand change. Where it is the government's fault then the actions Wikileaks took can be justified especially where 3000 Americans had already died due to the government's previous acts.

575.   Wikileaks is the same as the founders of the thirteen Colonies.

576.   If Wikileaks is wrong, it follows that the founding fathers were too bad in revolting and exposing the British's oppressive acts.

577.   All they did is highlight what the government is doing and something in their position believe that is wrong and putting the lives of the Americans in danger. Again, I reiterate that if it wasn't for 9/11 then the government might have been justified in pointing to the Espionage Act but 9/11 justifies the exposure of contributory acts by the government that are putting the lives of Americans in danger.

578.   An information revolution of this kind given the circumstances is justified because the American government through its soldiers was committing war crimes in Iraq. The fact that the exposure highlighted wrongdoings on the part of the government can exonerate Wikileaks in that one way or another other courts would have asked for the same material. In that way the government would have been compelled to release such information.

579.   Wikileaks can argue that one way or the other the courts would have requested this material or confessions from soldiers in the future. In that case, exposure now would have made little impact as the material would come out anywhere. Therefore Wikileaks could not be held accountable or much weight be put on the release of the material.

580.   The effects of the release of the material.

581.   Accusations of war crimes will no matter what follow a war, an invasion, or any military operation. The release of the material might not have changed the perception of the people. This is proved by 9/11. Wikileaks can argue that 9/11 made it public knowledge that the US government was ill-treating people abroad through its foreign policy. Surely no one can pretend to say that the American government was an angel after witnessing the kind of revenge and destruction aimed by the terrorists. It can be argued that the failed attack on the pentagon itself was a clear determination and argument by the terrorists

that the American government was wrong in treating foreigners abroad.

582.   Surely such acts are associated with evil and the terrorist explained why they were so determined to destroy everything American. They accused American foreign policy as the trigger of such hatred. So, the release of the material only justified what was already known. That the Americans are killing foreigners unjustly in what can be regarded as war crimes.

583.   After the release, most people would not be shocked by the video as it was already common knowledge. Releasing it or not was not going to change people's perceptions.

584.   Wikileaks position.

585.   9/11 introduced new perceptions and fears. The fact that Wikileaks was established after 9/11 it can be argued that 9/11 shifted the emphasis from secrecy to the need to protect the American people. It does not matter whether Wikileaks aimed to expose the government to trigger a change to protect Americans or not. Their acts can be said to have protected the Americans from another horrific 9/11. Even if that was not their intention. The release of the material can be said to have encouraged the scrutiny of the practices of that time. Could also have restrained the soldiers from further killings. Especially the fact that all knew from then that their acts could be exposed.

586.   Wikileaks is in a position in which they could know exactly the reasons for such attacks like 9/11 through their secret sources. It can be said to have felt obligated to stop such acts as 9/11 in an effort to trigger debate, scrutiny and further protection of the American people.

587.   Need to set legal precedence or trigger debates where government actions or foreign policy is responsible for harm that befalls the American people.

588.   Where a government is abusive and oppresses civil liberties and attacks the people's democratic rights like free

speech and freedom from imprisonment etc then some actions out of the norm are needed to effect change. Imagine if no one stood up to unjust and oppressive governments then humanity would have stopped existing and evolving. Imagine if the founding fathers obeyed all laws then [imagine that the Espionage Act was established there during the founding fathers' time.] Now imagine all listening to the oppressive British government and obeying this Espionage Act.

589.	Surely America wouldn't be here. Some acts are needed for humanity to evolve to the next stage of development. If a government is bringing harm to its people through its foreign policy and all having witnessed 9/11 and with this event attributed to the government's acts surely anyone with that kind of information will use it if that means stopping events like 9/11.

590.	I argue that if it wasn't for 9/11 and the circumstances surrounding 9/11 then the US government could have had a strong case against the Wikileaks founder. 9/11 renders any legal proceedings against the founder null and void. The government is the one to blame.

591.	Wikileaks can successfully argue that it wasn't for the government who brought all this upon the people. Not only that but the fact that they are still doing the same thing the terrorists cited as having triggered their revenge attacks. As such the government must be stopped and the only way is to expose them. Not to punish them as they could have lodged criminal proceedings against the government with the courts. But as a way to demand change and indirectly actually protect the American citizens from further revengeful attacks.

592.	The release of the material could have made the would-be terrorists to drop their plans to attack hoping that now that concrete evidence was released then the courts or other international communities might rebuke the government and make them stop the illegal killings. So, the release of the material could have protected the American people.

593.   The release could have triggered change or provided material to set up precedence where there is no absolute government power. This could have curtailed the power of government and given more power to the people who can expose a corrupt government without fear of being targeted. All in the name of protecting the American people. Even if they did not intend that, the fact that this can lead to a change in foreign policy means indirect protection of the American people.

594.   Investigative Journalism as a protection mechanism.

595.   It does not matter who releases the materials, whether it's Bradley Manning or Wikileaks. Where a government is involved in a foreign policy that is bringing harm to its people. The harm that has already been felt by the American people is the worst terrorist in history. The 9/11 attacks were felt globally that citizens or people of other nations felt obligated to expose such acts to protect against further harm being suffered by the American people.

596.   Where a government goes on to change its foreign policy. Where it changes how its soldiers deal with foreigners in war zones only after the exposure then the investigative journalists must be freed and cleared of any wrongdoings. This is because of their actions even if it appears that all this was malicious. The fact that change only came about through the release of the materials then they have protected the American people from its government.

597.   Considering the 9/11 attacks the investigative journalists can be entitled to compensation if wrongly imprisoned. The USA's case is special in that surely anyone would do anything to avoid 9/11. As such it is our position that all charges be dropped against the investigative journalists who escalated the situation to trigger debates and protection of the American people.

598.   We believe the reason why the government is going after these is to distract anyone who might be thinking of lodging war crimes criminal charges with the courts.

599.   We believe the only reason the government went after these is the fact that if they exonerate these they would be admitted to wrongdoing. So, keeping a tail on these shifts the blame from them to these. But the period that has elapsed can ease this complication in that now the government can easily forgive these and drop all charges knowing that no one will threaten to launch legal war crime proceedings against them. In that regard we as Tomorrow's World Order demand all charges be dropped against Julian Assange, Wikileaks, and everyone associated with this case.

600.   Investigative Journalism as a citizen protection mechanism regarding the dangers of a nuclear conflict and heightened risks of a World War Three.

601.   The fact that now countries have armed themselves with nuclear weapons and the bad foreign policy of governments means heightened risks of a nuclear war that will destroy cities and their inhabitants. Investigative Journalism in such a way has been given paramount importance in that such acts can curtail the government's negative influence abroad and lessen the risks of a nuclear war.

602.   We as Tomorrow's World Order are against any wars that kill women and children. We also believe that governments might not know the actions of their soldiers abroad. Or might not be tough with their soldiers because no one will ever know what they do abroad. So much release of material can be beneficial in protecting the people.

603.   Release of the material can act as a deterrent.

604.   This can lessen the effects of war. This can involve other international players who can condemn the war. They can make others get involved to stop the war or try to contain the effects of the war. The Russia-Ukraine war is a

perfect example. Imagine we as the new global leaders know that the West is going back in time to the 1665–1667 Anglo-Dutch war and using the same script through proxy war and letting Ukraine fight the Russians.

605.   See our Russia/Ukraine War Prediction.

606.   https://play.google.com/store/books/details/David_ Gomadza_A_Perfect_Prediction_Russia_Ukraine?id=Pma VEAAAQBAJ&gl=GB

607.   A Perfect Prediction: Russia Ukraine War/Military Operation by David Gomadza — Books on Google Play

608.   A Perfect Prediction: Russia Ukraine War/Military Operation — eBook written by David Gomadza. Read this book using the Google Play Books app on your PC, android, and iOS devices. Download for offline reading, highlight, bookmark or take notes while you read A Perfect Prediction: Russia Ukraine War/Military Operation.

609.   play.google.com

610.   Imagine the war going stage by stage, event by event as the war was then in 1665–1667 and with the possibilities and risks of Russia escalating the situation to de-escalate it through a tactical nuclear weapon.

611.   Now consider the obstinacy and resilience of the Ukraine government and on the other side the frustrations of Russia as a nuclear weapon-possessing state. Surely you can see easily how things can turn bad. We have precedence. The US and their ally the UK were put in such a position by the Japanese's obstinacy and ended up dropping not just one but two bombs. Many argue that this evil act catapulted the US to the top spot of the leader of the world.

612.   Now consider Russia having created the world's most destructive nuclear bomb the Tsar Bomb and the need to take power from the US in the east. Witnessed by recent challenges by Russia and China. If the US got the respect as the world's leader through spreading fear by dropping bombs. If Russia is to take the spot, then it follows also that

they must do evil to Ukraine. Now consider the West escalating the situation by supplying weapons surely if a superpower with a nuclear arsenal like Russia is defeated by a small country like Ukraine.

613.	To maintain their position and deter others from viewing them as weak might use nuclear weapons to maintain that superpower position. The idea of making nuclear weapons is to command the respect of smaller nations. If they can't do so then there are high risks that can fall into existential threats. A cornered animal is a dangerous animal.

614.	Having said that, publications of materials in this case just like after 9/11 is an obligation and the investigative journalists are there to play an important role in the safeguarding of peace and humanity at large.

615.	It would be absurd to go after an investigative journalist in this regard when they are acting in good faith to correct a wrong.

616.	Duty to the public and humanity at large.

617.	Investigative Journalism is an act to correct wrongdoing.

618.	Investigative Journalism in this case is critical in the need to trigger anti-war movements or critical movements that will campaign and push the government to change. Their acts are necessary to trigger change. To stir a revolution. State persecution and political victimisation by the government are not just illegal but unjust and must be opposed in every instance.

619.	They use the pledges of allegiance or oath of allegiance to make sure you won't tell until bad things start happening to you.

620.	I can argue that the hospital services are behind this they are the only ones whom people can trust. The only ones to use doctors to implant chips or fire a diode inside the bodies. Picture a nail gun. They are the ones recreating history. Using 1660s scripts to look for similar look-alikes and recreate events. This time we cornered them. Please download the Russia and Ukraine war Prediction by David Gomadza free on Google Play and see how accurate our prediction is. Word and event for event using the 1665–1667 Anglo-Dutch War. Proof that they are finding solutions to current problems way back in the 1660s.

621. https://play.google.com/store/books/details/David_Gomadza_A_Perfect_Prediction_Russia_Ukraine?id=Pma VEAAAQBAJ&gl=GB

622. The element of surprise and predictability and the competitive advantage. Right now, the Ukrainian President might be thinking that he is going to win the war soon. But the West is waiting for the war to end in July 2024. We intervened to stop this calculated murder plan. Mind you we stand against the killings of women and children.

623. So, are the British involved in all this?

624. The British might have indirectly tricked both Manning and Assange. It is a fact that Manning has Welsh therefore England connections

625. Britain had a protectionist treaty with the Kingdom of Saudi. Where they let them do their work and then give them protection. If they can falsify the dossier used to justify the war, then they can also actually trigger the terror attacks indirectly.

626. This is through an If-Then approach. As I said they might have directly or indirectly. I proved it is possible they might have used a script from the 1200s to 1660. They document all documents since the 1066 census. Only the British know of such material and how they do it. A knight as an achievement would in the end own a lot of wealth, lands, etc. Manning's parents were ordinary without enough wealth to live for her.

627. All this is based on the life of William Marshall Earl of Pembroke. The knight tournament games centred around making a profit. The fact that he/she might have contacted the New York Times possibly to sell the data.

Just speculation only as influenced by the instances of being a knight. But again, having grown up in Wales and the British system of hacking everyone digitally by secret implants she might have been tortured to defect and expose the American. This would help Britain. As the published materials implicated the Americans rather than the British. This is allegiance to the queen.

628.   In the Assange case.

629.   The fact that they would imprison him for such a long time without charges or a fair trial is suspect. What do the British lose if he is free? He is in a maximum-security prison. Is it to silence him? After all the charges by Sweden have since been dropped yet the British government is hanging onto him. Assange came to England to claim political asylum yet the British imprisoned him. Could all the suggestions above fill the gap as to the real reasons behind their imprisonment of him?

630.   As a political refugee, the British had no right to imprison him, especially for such a long time. After all, he came to Britain to seek political asylum.

631.   Above all, according to the UK of parliament page, four of the original Magna Carta that protect individual rights are still in force as law'

632.   Here I will quote only clause 39 and 40 relevant here.

633.   "No free man shall be seized, imprisoned, dispossessed, outlawed, exiled or ruined in any way, nor in any way proceeded against, except by the lawful judgement of his peers and the law of the land.

634.   "To no one, will we sell, to no one will we deny or delay right or justice."

635.   *UK parliament laws. Magna Carta.*

636.   The issues raised in this case pose serious implications for freedoms and liberties where a government wrongly believes in its divine right. I have argued in my

recent book CABAL SKRPT [1665–1667 script] A Stories Prediction.

637.   FREE DOWNLOAD

638.   https://play.google.com/store/books/details/David_ Gomadza_CABAL_SKRPT_1665_70s_script_A_Storie?id =JWCdEAAAQBAJ&gl=GB

639.   That the Tories were formed in the 1660s and more than often go back in time and recreate events then use the 1660s script to rewrite and shape history. At the time in question, the King believed in the divine right of the government. Where the king chose to put aside arguments to consider personal liberties over his divine right. Here in 2022, we see the Tories abandoning international laws in favour of the government's right to make all laws and choose which ones they can abide by. But the issue as explained in this book is the fact that they are taking 2022 to the 1660s and finding solutions that imitate and help recreate the 1660s.

640.   Then abused everyone. They are secretly tortured people into submission. Now they are heavily investing in digital technology to chip everyone and enforce remote submission and control of the people. Something we are against hence the current issues. The government is so fixed in the 1660s that they can't see life from other people's view.

641.   So, we believe that they are holding Assange as a way to silence him until he dies in prison, something we are against. It is not just immoral and unjustified for the UK having the above Magna Carta clauses as operation and as law. To hold Assange for such a long time without the right to justice. The United Nations confirmed that the Iraq war was illegal. We can argue that Britain falsified dossiers to entice America to go to war.

642.   Above all, they are the ones through advanced digital technology who are behind terrorists' activities where they trick terrorists through deep sleep digital technology and whispering of playback recordings deep

into the inner ear as an inner voice by reducing the sound decibels. So that when a person hears this small voice, he will think it's a dream as the brain since it is his own voice will convert audio to pictures so the person dreams this.

643. Read my books that explain how they are doing this.

644. Thoughts to Word or Audio by David Gomadza.

645. https://play.google.com/store/books/details/David_Gomadza_Thoughts_To_Word_Or_Audio?id=q2xmEAAAQBAJ&gl=GB

646. Decoding Thoughts and Inner Voice. Explanations and Debunking the Inner Voice by David Gomadza.

647. https://play.google.com/store/books/details/David_Gomadza_Decoding_Thoughts_and_Inner_Voice_Ex?id=qi1qEAAAQBAJ&gl=GB

648. Britain cannot say that they will hold Assange for the Americans, especially in prison. The time he has spent in jail is unjustified and as such, we demand his release before Christmas.

649. The arguments used against the US government also apply to the UK government. He exposed both for war crimes. The UN declared the war as illegal. The international criminal court could have investigated these if it wasn't for the sanctions against the court officials.

650. They dropped the charges in 2009.

651. So, either way, the material could have been released to the courts if the same information was discovered through the court system. That exonerates Assange. The fact that Magna Carta's is in force especially the two clauses 39 and 40 which are relevant in this case only points to abuse by the UK government in which case we believe Assange is entitled to compensation and apology and immediate release without any conditions. We argue that the UK should have given Assange political

asylum rather than a prison term. Unless they have something to hide.

652.   The UK government's guilt of falsifying documents triggers the trickery that caused Manning and Assange to release the documents they have falsified so as to clear their name and reputation. It is logical to think this way after all he spent years in British jail. Probably the have a lot to cover.

653.   It can be argued that shame fell on the British after the Iraq war for their role in falsifying dossiers that were used to invade Iraq. Now to cover their tracks they now entice or trick through the oath of allegiance or pledge of allegiance to make Manning and Assange publish documents that the US government even if that happened after the 9/11 attacks will use to justify all evil acts and their actions thereafter as if the release and publications happened first. This could be the reason they are relying on and justifying holding Assange in prison.

654.   We are against such thinking. We argue that the practice of these going back to the 1660s can be the sole reason why they think Assange should still be in jail. This is a deranged form of thinking which we oppose firmly in this case because they have blood on their hands of civilian deaths in Iraq nearing around 1 million casualties.

655.   We argued that they gained as well financially as they announced only a day after the beheading of Sadden Hussein that they were now in a position to repay the debt they owed the USA going back as far as WWII.

656.   But we argue that the continual holding of Assange in prison is no longer justified considering the time that has elapsed. Then it could be understood that the government was protecting its soldiers by his imprisonment without charges as a deterrent to others who might be willing to take the soldiers to court. The long time that has elapsed surely removes any basis by this government to hold him in prison as such must be released asap.

657.   The International Court's stance on war crimes.

658.   Legality of the War.

659.   *The 2003 invasion of Iraq by the United States,
United Kingdom, Australia, Poland, and a coalition of
other countries was a violation of the United Nations
Charter, the bedrock of international relations in the post-
World War II world. The then United Nations Secretary-
General Kofi Annan stated in September 2004 that: "I have
indicated it was not in conformity with the UN charter.
From our point of view and the UN Charter point of view,
it [the war] was illegal".[1][2]*
660.   *Wikipedia.*

661.   US and UK officials have argued that existing UN
Security Council resolutions related to the 1991 Gulf War
and the subsequent ceasefire (660, 678), and to later
inspections of Iraqi weapons programs (1441), had already
authorised the invasion. [9] Critics of the invasion have
challenged both of these assertions, arguing that an
additional Security Council resolution, which the US and
UK failed to obtain, would have been necessary to
specifically authorise the invasion
662.   Wikipedia.
663.   *In 2020 the ICC concluded that it was dropping its
case against the UK for possible war crimes committed
between 2003 and 2008. Not because the UK soldiers were
innocent. But ICC prosecutor Fatou Bensouda announced
the decisions even as she admitted there was a "reasonable
basis to believe" that British armed forces may have
carried out atrocities, including the wilful killing of
detainees held in custody in Iraq between 2003 and 2008.*
664.   *The ICC refuses to prosecute UK war crimes in
Iraq despite "reasonable" evidence*
665.   *The International Criminal Court (ICC) has
abandoned its inquiry into war crimes committed by British
troops in Iraq...*
666.   *www.wsws.org*

667.   The ICC prosecutor believed that ...the evidence in some cases was so damning that in 2014 ICC prosecutor Fatou Bensouda had accepted a complaint alleging UK military personnel had committed war crimes against Iraqis in their custody between 2003 and 2008 and ordered a preliminary investigation.

668.   *The article goes on to state the British tactics of stalling investigations later evidenced by their legislation proposing a five-year limit on prosecutions for soldiers serving outside the UK. The Overseas Operations (Service Personnel and Veterans) Bill creates a "presumption against prosecution" that gives the green light to future war crimes, including torture and the mass murder of civilians.*

669.   It can be argued that such treatment of their soldiers should also cover Assange's case that he be released without any crimes against him.

670.   It is a sad fact that the UK was concealing their soldiers' crimes by going after Assange as a deterrent to others to investigate the crimes. This Overseas Bill protects the soldiers therefore there is no justification for holding Assange.

671.   It contrasts starkly with Britain's treatment of Wiki-leaks journalist and publisher Julian Assange. Assange's only "crime" was to expose war crimes — including killings, torture, abuse — regime-change operations, and global spying committed by the US and its allies, including Britain. In the eyes of the ruling class, investigative journalists, not the perpetrators, are the real criminals. Assange sits in London's maximum-security Belmarsh Prison, dubbed the UK's Guantánamo Bay — amid the spread of COVID-19 throughout the facility — as the US seeks his extradition to face jail for life, if not execution, on US Espionage Act charges.

672.   The fact that the ICC dropped charges on British war crimes justifies the dropping of this Assange case and his immediate release. The fact that the ICC was eager to open war crimes cases against British soldiers justifies

Assange's actions in that one way or the other the courts will come for the same materials and evidence. So technically it doesn't matter who released and published the material. Assange published the materials as an escalation to de-escalate tactic in aiming to protect the American people from the reckless outsourcing of terror and deaths of their own citizens by the US government.

673.   The continual imprisonment of Assange without charges can only highlight UK's implications and involvement not just in the war but in the 9/11 terror attacks. The UK is holding Assange to stop him from revealing who might be behind the 9/11 terror attacks themselves. Revisit our going back to the 1660s by the UK as a way of finding solutions. But I argued also that even if the solution worked in the 1660s surely a lot has changed.

674.

You can't argue that if Larry Silverstone had approached the British NHS or American health system etc for a solution to the huge costs of running the twin towers, the change in the law in the use of asbestos in buildings, and the huge demolition costs they would simply have said yes we can use the 1660s script and recreate a modified version of the great fire of London mixed with the destruction of the Sodom and Gomorrah. Even if it is likely that something similar happened. Picture Judy Giuliani as the mayor of New York and all his efforts to put the fire out and compare that to the role of Simon Pepys during the Great fire of London.

675.   Surely the UK has more to hide. We argue that since they have protected the real culprits who committed the crimes Assange exposed, it followed too that if that is to remain that way then Assange must be released as well. He served enough time in prison that whatever crime he might have been portioned to is served.

676.   Mind you his crime was revealing the crimes the British committed. If they can defer any scrutiny, they must

release Assange and apply the same principle otherwise that legislation is null and void.

677.   Bensouda stated that Britain had set up the Iraq Historic Allegations Team (IHAT) in 2010 in response to the "admitted failures of the British army at the time to conduct effective investigations." IHAT investigated 3,405 war crimes allegedly committed by British troops during the occupation of Iraq between 2003 and 2009. But despite evidence of widespread abuse and mistreatment, including the killing of unarmed civilians and children, she noted that no charges had been brought against any soldiers — "a result that has deprived the victims of justice."

678.   We understand the circumstances as well surrounding the war. Probably a one-off situation and also as such we argue that Assange must be released for all he did is pinpoint the wrongdoing in an escalate-to de-escalate the situation. As such is a free man. The UK is under a huge obligation to release Assange in the name of justice.

679.   We strongly believe that the UK is holding Assange as blackmail and as ransom to the USA in that if Assange is wrong in exposing the US government just as the founding fathers' rebellion. Then the UK has a strong case against the US. In that case to prove a point they are simply going to hold Assange to his death, something they could have done to the founding fathers using treason acts [Espionage Act].

680.   The US to protect the American people, the constitution, and the history of the founding fathers they must with immediate effect drop all charges against Assange.

681.   This will point to the UK's illegality in dealing with Assange. Right now, the UK is relying on the USA sending through the extradition orders. If it wasn't for this Sweden had dropped its case and that meant that the UK had no basis for holding Assange. The threats by the US are giving the UK every right to abuse Assange but as a ransom for the fact that the US is like Assange and therefore punishable by their courts. The very reason that we think the UK just to prove a point will not release Assange.

682.   So, we demand that the US take a look at themselves first before pointing fingers and act right. Drop all charges against Assange otherwise, the UK has everything against you.

683.   Your constitution is based on what Assange is fighting for. In England, the Magna Carta clause relevant to the issue at hand is still in force. Even if the US doesn't recognise this here in the UK the US [if the US does not drop the charges] will keep holding Assange without trial.

684.   We as the new global leaders are against such thinking. The US is literally shooting itself in the foot.

685.   Drop all charges against Assange and proof to the UK that you are serious about the freedoms and rights of individuals.

686.   Assange is your George Washington.

687.   Assange is your Thomas Jefferson.

688.   Assange is your John Adams.

689.   Assange is your Benjamin Franklin

690.   Assange is your Alexander Hamilton

691.   Assange is your John Kay

692.   Assange is your James Madison

693.   Assange is your living constitution

694.   Assange is your American pride.

695.   Assange is your personal liberties.

696.   Assange is your living proof that America is great. That America is a land of the free. That America is the dream country.

697.   If not for your pride then do it for future generations for, we are against recolonisation, holding people to ransom, and all kinds of evil.

698.   FREE MEANS FREE.

699.   DON'T GIVE UP EVERYTHING TO COLONIAL THINKING.

700.   Surely you can't tell me that the founders fought for nothing and that you cowards give everything back to Britain just because the caveman Osama Bin Laden threatens to kill America? I would sacrifice 100 000 men for one inch of that freedom. For the inch of personal liberties.

701.   Where are you going wrong? Have you become hostages as well to recolonisation? Are they threatening to take your loved ones unless you obey?

702.   I think there is no justification for giving up what you stand for. Others gave up their lives so that the world is a better place.

703.   What will you tell:

704.   George Washington?

705.   Thomas Jefferson?

706.   John Adams?

707.   Benjamin Franklin?

708.   Alexander Hamilton?

709.   John Kay?

710.   James Madison?

711.   That you were so scared of the terrorists that you gave your personal liberties away? That you are going now with Britain recolonising the world like barbarians. Imprisoning people for years in Guantanamo without the right to justice. I believe 9/11 was the most horrific event in American history but that is just a test. Would you give up everything for a piece of stolen land like Chagos?

712.   We have reasons to believe that to the British; America was simply leased to you just as they did with the Chagos.

713.   Surely the implications of that threaten the fabric of American society and existence more than the acts of terrorists.

714.   Terrorists destroy builds and kill people but will never take away hard-earned freedoms but recolonisation and barbaric thinking will.

715.   Technically you Espionage Acts do not hold water. It's outdated and when it was written things were different then. Do you know that then there were no terrorists? After all, we all know now that you love the 1660s very much. Technically you are using outdated laws.

716.   The best opportunity to change. To write new laws that are fit for modern times.

717.   Open your eyes.

718.   Do the right thing. Your boys and girls are safe. It's time to let this man go free forever.

719.   What is happening right now is not the American dream. We understand what was at stake then. The fear of the unknown. The fear of 9/11 and the fear of the existential threat that terrorists can pose. But let us all learn from our mistakes. If you can forgive your men, your women, and soldiers who did the war crimes no matter what reason you can forgive Assange.

720.   All he did was tell the world what your boys were doing. Not for them to be punished but to effect change. I don't know of any court papers Assange lodged against your boys and girls he lodges with the ICC because he is not after your boys and girls.

721.   He is like Tomorrow's World Order. We just want a fair and just system. A system that works for everyone. Okay, you can be forgiven for not knowing what was happening in Iraq. But he made you aware. He did not threaten them with death. No. Nor did he wish them bad luck.

722.   All he did was wish them to become better soldiers. They become better people so as to avoid the courts and future war crimes. All this because he cares about justice. He cares about righting a wrong. As such let us start afresh. Your boys and girls are safe and untouched ever since the release of the materials as such. We now demand his release simply because all your boys and girls are free. Whatever sin he committed he served time and must be released asap.

723.   We as Tomorrow's World Order since not any of the accused were dragged to court likewise; we have exonerated him. We grant him pardon whether you put conditions for a limited time as a condition to release him immediately that is up to you.

724.   Don't be tricked into recolonisation of countries and personal liberties due to fear of terrorists. There is no country that has a near to perfect justice system than the US or was. Keep that reputation, don't be dragged into wars and abuse of people's rights.

725.   Let's start afresh.
726.   FREE ASSANGE TODAY!!!
727.   I am the new first global president.
728.   The heightened risks of a nuclear war between
     Russia and Ukraine have highlighted the need for a new
     global order. We can't leave things to chance anymore.
729.   Signed
730.   07 December 2022
731.   David Gomadza
732.   The First Global President.
733.   info@twofuture.world
734.   00447863020828
735.   www.twofuture.world.
736.

FREE JULIAN ASSANGE Escalate-to-Deescalate

DAVID GOMADZA

The First Global President
00447863020828
info@twofuture.world
www.twofuture.world

www.ingramcontent.com/pod-product-compliance
Lightning Source LLC
Chambersburg PA
CBHW051353280526
45784CB00007B/2940